Theory and Reality
in International Relations

Theory and Reality
in International Relations

EDITED BY

JOHN C. FARRELL AND ASA P. SMITH

COLUMBIA UNIVERSITY PRESS

NEW YORK AND LONDON

Foreword

The pragmatic bent of Americans, their bias against the theoretical and abstract and in favor of the practical and concrete, is a commonplace. Lionel Trilling in *The Liberal Imagination* put it well:

> In the American metaphysic, reality is always material reality, hard, resistant, unformed, impenetrable, and unpleasant. And that mind is alone felt to be trustworthy which most resembles this reality by most nearly reproducing the sensations it affords.

In this view, theorizing only serves to obscure reality, to distract the observer from the "hard, cold facts" that alone will enable him to grasp reality. It is such a notion of reality and the way it is apprehended that lies behind the argument, frequently heard today, that only those privy to the facts available to a government's policy-makers can fairly criticize their policies. Consideration of the current Vietnam debate reveals the flaw in that argument; for while the facts (as far as they can be ascertained) are certainly relevant, the argument over the wisdom of this country's military involvement in Vietnam really revolves around conflicting images, concepts, and theories about contemporary international relations. The difference between a critic of the war like Hans Morgenthau and a defender like Walt Rostow is more a matter of conflicting *Weltanschauungs* than of a disagreement over the facts.

We are concerned with man's apprehension of the reality of the nations and the interactions between them that constitute international relations. In the companion volume, *Image and Reality in World Politics*, we point up how inevitably subjective is man's attempt to make sense of the world. Apprehending reality in international relations, as in anything else, is not simply a matter of amassing more and more facts, of somehow reproducing in one's mind a factual configuration of external reality. Rather, recent social-psychological research suggests that man's effort to comprehend reality is greatly influenced by the cognitive structure or image through which the data are mediated and ordered. Without this mental organization, this subjective shaping of reality, the data of international relations would be like Macbeth's description of life: ". . . a tale told by an idiot, full of sound and fury, signifying nothing."

Images necessarily distort reality. That is what makes them functional. The attempt to apprehend the reality of the structure and processes of international relations, resulting in conceptual or theoretical "images" functionally similar to the everyday images through which the average man makes sense of the world, also involves a distortion of reality.[1] As James Rosenau points out in a recent review essay of his,[2] the observer seeking to understand the universe of international-relations phenomena "must select in order to know reality, and in so doing he must distort it. He must use some method to comprehend the truth of world politics, thus inevitably rendering it subjective." Once it is realized that a theoretical statement of the way things are in international relations is simply a specialized image, then the "realistic" objection to theory as such is seen to be irrelevant.

The question, then, is not theory *or* reality but theory *and* reality. The articles in this book—whether they deal with the nature of theoretical understanding and the limits reality imposes on it, or discuss the consequences for foreign policy when an accepted theoretical image bears little relation to reality, or show how changes in historical reality call forth new theoretical concepts, or discuss how normative theory can be relevant to the ethical dilemmas with which reality confronts the statesman, or show what good theory is by actually theorizing—are collectively designed to illuminate that relationship.

[1] For an interesting development of this analogy between image-building and theory-formulating, see Charles A. McClelland, *Theory and the International System* (New York: The Macmillan Co., 1966), Ch. 1.

[2] James Rosenau, "Games International-Relations Scholars Play," *Journal of International Affairs*, Vol. XXI, No. 2 (1967), p. 295.

Contents

Theory and Reality
in International Relations

RAYMOND ARON

What Is a Theory of
International Relations?

Few words are used as often by economists, sociologists, or political scientists as the word "theory." Few are as ambiguous. A recent book developing two ideas—the virtues of non-alignment and the influence that the priority of economic considerations in modern societies allegedly exerts in favor of peace—has as its subtitle "general theory."[1] A hypothesis that alliances are founded on calculations of national interest and do not withstand a conflict of those interests is christened "theory" in the current language of political science.[2] As a matter of fact, the distinction is rarely explicitly made between related but distinct concepts such as "model," "ideal type," "conceptualization," and even an empirically observed regular occurrence. What authors call "theory" belongs more or less to one or the other of these categories, or may contain elements borrowed from one or the other in varying proportions.

This lack of rigor in the use of a key word can be explained and perhaps justified by the desire for progress. Political scientists feel that their dis-

---

[1] J. W. Burton, *International Relations: A General Theory* (Cambridge: Cambridge University Press, 1965).
[2] Raymond Dawson and Richard Rosecrance, "Theory and Reality in the Anglo-American Alliance," *World Politics*, Vol. XIX, No. 1 (Oct. 1966), pp. 21-51.

Raymond Aron is professor of sociology at the Sorbonne. He is the author of *Peace and War: A Theory of International Relations, The Great Debate, Century of Total War, the Dawn of Universal History, France: Steadfast and Changing, France: the New Republic, German Sociology, Introduction to the Philosophy of History, On War, The Opium of the Intellectuals,* and *War and Industrial Society.*

cipline appears underdeveloped compared to economics, not to mention the natural sciences. This desire for progress has the unfortunate effect of making it seem more important to do than to know what one is doing. The accumulation of information matters more than the critical understanding of it.

However, the quarrel between proponents of the "classical" and "scientific" approaches to the study of international relations, a quarrel I deplore because it has increased the confusion, shows that scholars in the field are not indifferent to the theoretical basis of their discipline. Thus, perhaps it will not be entirely useless to pose the question: What is a theory of international relations?

I

It seems to me that in the Western world the concept of theory has a double origin or, if you prefer, two meanings, each derived from a different tradition. Theory as contemplative knowledge, drawn from ideas or from the basic order of the world, can be the equivalent of philosophy. In that case, theory differs not only from practice or action, but from knowledge animated by the will to "know in order to predict and thus be able to act." The less practical a study is, the less it suggests or permits the handling of its object, the more theoretical it is. At most, it changes the one who has conceived it and those who are enlightened by it through his findings.

The other line of thought leads to authentically scientific theories, with those of physical science offering the perfect model. In this sense, a theory is a hypothetical, deductive system consisting of a group of hypotheses whose terms are strictly defined and whose relationships between terms (or variables) are most often given a mathematical form. The elaboration of this system starts with a conceptualization of perceived or observed reality; axioms or highly abstract relationships govern the system and allow the scientist to rediscover by deduction either appearances that are thereby fully explained, or facts that are perceptible through devices, if not through the senses, and that temporarily either confirm the theory or invalidate it. An invalidation necessitates a rectification; a confirmation never constitutes an absolute proof of the theory's truth.

We shall entirely discard the first meaning, i.e., theory as philosophy, and restrict ourselves to the second meaning, the meaning preferred by the "modernists" among sociologists and political scientists.

Aside from the special case of linguistics, probably economics, of all the social sciences, has developed theoretical elaboration to the greatest extent. Pure economics, in the style of Walras and Pareto, constitutes the equivalent of a hypothetical, deductive system; it is expressed in a set of equations. But it is well known, as Walras and Pareto were the first to point out, that pure economics sets up a simplified representation of reality. In place of actual economic life the economist substitutes an artificial market where men of flesh and bones are replaced by subjects with specially defined characteristics. They have perfect information at their disposal and a single objective, the maximization of a certain quantity (the intervention of money makes this calculation easy).

It is not our concern here to enter into a classic controversy over whether economic models are comparable to the theory of rational mechanics or whether they should be considered as "ideal types" according to Max Weber's conception, that is, as rationalized and stylized reconstructions of certain types of behavior and situations. Although I personally prefer the second interpretation, it is not necessary to choose between them; indeed, both lead to the notions I should like to restate.

The models of pure economics provide indispensable insights (the reciprocal solidarity among all the elements of the system, the need for economic calculation in order to decide on a rational allocation of resources, the dependence of each price on all prices, etc.). Those without some theoretical training always run the risk of committing great errors if they limit themselves to empirical description or research. For example, they might predict a wave of unemployment with each spectacular technological innovation. But, in the opposite sense, theorists do not have the right to derive a doctrine of action from their models. The fact that the perfect market assures an optimum distribution of resources does not authorize the doctrinaire to claim that science demonstrates the superiority of free enterprise over socialism. Even if we ignore the fact that this distribution is optimum only for a certain distribution of income, the fact remains that pure theory carves out a clearly defined system (the economy) within an undefined system (the global society) and defines an imaginary actor (*homo oeconomicus*) far removed from real actors. (It is not true that all behavior that deviates from that of the imaginary actors disappears in the mass and that average behavior or the final outcome of real behavior corresponds to the expectations based exclusively on behavior as defined by the theory, that is, on behavior aiming at a maximum gain.)

Progress in economic science results from a ceaseless dialectic between theory and experiments. The theory in operation today has been profoundly marked by the influence of Keynes, whose "general theory" diverged sharply from classical theories in several respects: it was directly macro-economic; it set up six variables, some independent and some dependent (at the same time, it suggested a technique of manipulation); it considered equilibrium at the level of full employment as a special case; it set up an entrepreneur different from the economic subject of traditional theory, an entrepreneur who would make investment decisions based upon expected profit (individual psychology, the psychological climate of the community, in other words social-psychological data, were thereby introduced into the system); and finally, it postulated, so to speak, the non-elasticity of nominal wages, thereby integrating additional social data into the system.

One could debate whether Keynesian theory is a general theory or just a model valid for explaining short-term fluctuations and their control for a historical period characterized by certain extra-economic factors. I shall not undertake this discussion, which would be an excessively long digression in view of the aims of this short essay. Indeed, the preceding discussion should suggest the following propositions that have implications for the study of international relations.

1) In order to elaborate the theory of a social sub-system, we need a definition of this sub-system that defines both its limits and its specificity. What are the true characteristics of the interconnected actions that constitute a relatively defined whole, whose implicit logic the theory tries to elaborate?

2) Scientific progress requires shuttling back and forth between simplified systems and renewed observations. Keynes' system involves actors who are less remote from actual actors than those in Walras' system. At the same time, Keynes postulates certain historical and social facts outside the specific field of economics (external variables).

3) Even the Keynesian system assumes the constancy of data that, in reality, are not constant; focusing on short-term fluctuations, Keynes does not take technical progress into consideration.

4) Progress in the economic field over the past thirty years has been largely due to empirical, statistical, and descriptive studies. Empirical and statistical studies have led to an awareness of essential phenomena, such as long-term growth and the transformation of price relationships among goods of different sectors owing to unequal rates of growth in productivity. National accounting, much more than theory, has given governments better control over economic fluctuations. Models of crisis—the configurations of variables considered as crisis indicators—have been misleading; indeed, it has not yet been proven that "crisis situations" are all alike. It is possible that each crisis is unique or, if you prefer, has its own particular story, and that the structure of the system itself contains possibilities of a crisis.

5) Progress in economic knowledge has not eliminated doctrinal conflicts, uncertainties in short- or middle-term forecasting, or the political (in other words partisan) dimension of the decisions taken by governments (decisions affecting the interests of various social classes in various ways). In short, neither theoretical knowledge nor empirical findings authorize the economist to dictate, in the name of science, a specific action to a ruler, although he can often advise the ruler on how to avoid evils dreaded by the whole community and sometimes predict the probable consequences of the ruler's actions. We cannot go directly from theory as a science to theory as a doctrine for action.

From these propositions emerge the problems I should like to raise about the theory of international relations.

1) Is it possible, and if so how, to define and delimit the sub-system of international relations?

2) What is the relation of this theory to empirical study, of the sub-system to the social context? Is this theory historical or meta-historical? (This question was debated by the marginalist and historicist schools of economic thought at the end of the nineteenth century.)

3) What are the connections between theory and doctrine or, to use a word that shocked so many American readers, between theory and praxeology.[3]

Thus we rediscover the classical antitheses that define the meaning of theory: reality and theory, empiricism (historical and sociological) and theory, practice and theory.

II

We can determine the true field of international relations in two ways. Either we try to grasp what distinguishes this field from other social fields, what differentiates relationships among politically organized communities from all other social relationships, or we start with concepts that can be applied to areas other than international relations. This difference in approach in no way corresponds to that between traditionalists and modernists. Hans Morgenthau is a traditionalist and Kenneth Boulding is a

[3] May I say, without being impertinent, that the reaction of American critics to the word *praxeology*, including that of my friend Henry Kissinger, who was in other respects so kindly disposed, seems typically parochial to me. Recalling the awkward jargon found on every page of sociological studies, one is amazed that a correctly composed word (praxis-logos), which has no equivalent (the science of practice) and is in current use in Europe (Professor Kotarbinski, Professor of the Polish Academy of Sciences, wrote a well-known book bearing this title), should offend a linguistic purism so rarely in evidence.

modernist, yet both begin with general concepts not unique to international relations: *power* and *conflict*. International power politics or international conflicts are treated as species belonging to a genus, as illustrations or special cases of universally human phenomena. The first pages of that classic, *Politics Among Nations*,[4] offer an equally classic example of conceptual confusion arising from the use of a term such as "power," which, depending on the paragraph or even the sentence one is reading, means either the end or the means of politics and which, finally, is of no use. If "power" is defined in Weber's way, which is moreover the common way, as the ability of agent A to get agent B to submit to his will or to obey his orders (or, more precisely, the good fortune of agent A to achieve submission and obedience), then all social life is a question of power to some extent; power is obviously essential for collective action in any field whatsoever. Setting up power, thus defined, as the unique and highest goal of individuals, parties, or nations does not constitute a theory in the scientific sense, but instead amounts to a philosophy or an ideology. In any event, it is not a proposition that can be proven false; thus it cannot even be considered a scientific hypothesis.

I chose the other alternative in my book *Paix et Guerre entre les Nations*.[5] I tried to determine what constituted the distinctive nature of international or interstate relations, and I concluded that it lay in the legitimacy or legality of the use of military force. In superior civilizations, these are the only social relationships in which violence is considered normal.

This conclusion was not at all original: it was obvious to the classical philosophers and to the jurists who developed European international law (*jus gentium*). It has been confirmed, if I may say so, by the experience of our century and by the failure of American statesmen. The latter, prisoners of the contradiction between a national ideology (that war is a crime and that the rule of law must prevail in the relations between nations) and the nature of international society, have appeared to others as cynical, naïve, or hypocritical. Never was the contradiction as glaring, and in a way both tragic and comic, as at the time of the double crisis in Hungary and Suez. To justify the stand taken against the British and French, President Eisenhower made the memorable remark, "There should not be two laws, one for friends, another for enemies" (the British and French were the friends), at the very time when he was passively witnessing the crushing

---

[4] Hans J. Morgenthau, *Politics Among Nations* (New York: Alfred Knopf, 1949).

[5] Translated into English as *Peace and War: A Theory of International Relations* by Richard Howard and Annette Baker Fox (Garden City, N.Y.: Doubleday and Co., 1966).

of the Hungarian revolution by Soviet troops. American friends told me later that they had felt moral pride upon learning that President Eisenhower was joining the Soviets and the Third World against the British and French "in the name of law." They did not want to admit that President Eisenhower,[6] in allowing the Soviet Union to do as it pleased in Eastern Europe, was devaluating the legal or moral significance of the UN censure of the Anglo-French expedition and was applying the old rule of the international jungle: there are two laws, one for the strong, another for the weak. The strong have not yet found a better means of avoiding conflict and imposing something approaching order than by defining spheres of influence.

In short, neither the Kellogg-Briand Pact nor the United Nations has as yet eliminated the basic characteristic of the international system that philosophers and jurists of previous centuries designated the "state of nature." They contrasted it with the civil state, which possessed a tribunal and a police force. There is no equivalent of a tribunal in international society; and if the United Nations tried to compel one of the great powers to submit against its will, the police action would degenerate into a major war. Furthermore, the UN Charter explicitly recognizes the "sovereign equality" of states, and diplomats have never succeeded in defining the "international crime" *par excellence*—aggression.

The Cuban missile crisis of 1962 provides the same lesson. Frederick II gave his lawyers the task of justifying, ex post facto, the conquest of Silesia. President Kennedy found lawyers to formulate the "quarantine" of Cuba in apparently legal terms. But all the legal subtleties could not hide an undeniable fact: the United States itself has continuously applied the principle that every government has the right to request the stationing of armed forces of another state on its territory if it judges this outside assistance necessary to its security. According to this principle, Cuba had as much right to set up Soviet medium-range missile bases as Turkey had to set up American bases. Fortunately, President Kennedy was not dissuaded by legal considerations. As Frederick had done, he consulted his lawyers for the apparent legitimization of a necessity. And the whole world is grateful to him for having strengthened the effectiveness of deterrence more in a few days than hundreds of books or speeches would have done in a dozen years. At the same time, that crisis, settled without the loss of hu-

---

[6] It goes without saying that these remarks are not meant as either an attack on or an approval of American policies in 1956. Maybe there was nothing better to do, but the moralizing speech, perhaps necessary for American public opinion, camouflaged a diplomacy that the European disciples of Machiavelli would not have repudiated.

man lives, marked a turning point in the postwar era; it hastened the liquidation of the Berlin affair and gave a new content to "peaceful coexistence" between the two superpowers. World opinion was grateful for the priority given to the exigencies of the balance of nuclear forces over the sovereign rights of a small country. Wiser than the ideologists, it took into account the circumstances and intentions rather than the law.

Can that essential characteristic—the absence of a tribunal or police force, the right to resort to force, the plurality of autonomous centers of decision, the alternation and continual interplay between peace and war[7]—serve as a basis for a scientific theory, even though it is obvious to the actors themselves and belongs to their own intuitive "sociology" or "political science"? Should not science substitute for everyday notions those concepts that science itself elaborates? It seems easy for me to answer that nothing prevents us from translating the preceding idea into a word or a formula more satisfactory to the "scientists." As we know, Max Weber defined the state as a "monopoly of legitimate violence." Let us say that international society is characterized by "the absence of an entity that holds a monopoly of legitimate violence."

A theoretical definition of this kind cannot be proven in the same way as an equation in theoretical physics: by showing its agreement with experimental data. Nor can it be invalidated. Even if a monopoly of legitimate violence in international society should be established in the future, we would merely say that the specific domain of interstate relations, as it had existed for a few thousand years, had disappeared as such. Yet a theoretical definition of this kind entails several direct and indirect confirmations. To simplify matters, I shall say that these confirmations will be brought forth by answering the following questions: (1) Does this definition permit the delimitation of the sub-system that is being considered? (2) Does it allow us to deduce or include other elements of the sub-system? (3) Does it permit us to rediscover (and to explain) the original data that served as a starting point for the theoretical elaboration?

The answer to the first question seems, on the whole, positive. I do not deny the difficulties involved. The real delimitation is often more difficult than the conceptual one. In primitive societies, it is sometimes hard to find the effective power that holds the highest authority. In the absence of politically and territorially organized entities, distinctions between various types of more or less violent conflict and between groups are vague. The collective actor that reserves for itself the right to use violence against other

---

[7] The formulas are not equivalent but can easily be deduced from each other.

collective actors is more or less large: a village, a clan, or a tribe. But the difficulty in defining sub-systems in primitive societies by using concepts derived from complex societies exists in economics as well as in international relations. Why blame the theory for what can be imputed to the very nature of its subject matter? Likewise, it would be easy to object that feudal societies, owing to the dispersion of means of combat, make it difficult to distinguish between violence within the state and violence between states. Civil wars, such as the American Civil War, are also often hard to distinguish from foreign wars. Moreover, international law has taken these marginal cases into account. When a state loses the "monopoly of legitimate violence," and two parties have organized military forces at their disposal, the non-belligerents tend to treat the two camps as if each one formed a separate state. However, such marginal cases do not constitute a valid objection to the rigor of the initial definition.

I believe that the answer to the second question provides the best justification for our chosen point of departure. Indeed, by postulating a society without a monopoly of legitimate violence, composed of collective actors, each of which confers the monopoly of legitimate violence on an entity within itself, we also implicitly define the main variables necessary to explain the systems and the events. As a matter of fact, the plurality of collective actors implies geographical space in two respects: the area in which each of the collective actors is established, and the area within which the relations between the actors take place. Actors whose mutual relations are such that each one takes all the others into account in the calculations preceding its decisions belong to the same system. In the absence of a monopoly of legitimate violence, each actor is obliged to provide for its own security, either with its own forces or by joining forces with its allies. Consequently, the configuration of forces (bipolar or multipolar) is one of the main variables of any international system. Since each actor is controlled, in its relations with the other actors, by the entity that possesses a monopoly of legitimate violence, and thus by the handful of men who are responsible for it, the internal regimes of the collective actors constitute one of the variables of the international system: the homogeneity or heterogeneity of the system depends upon the kinship or opposition between the internal regimes of the different actors.

Should such an analysis be called a *theory* or a *conceptualization*? Is it an outline of a theory or an admission that a general theory is impossible? It all depends on what we expect of a theory, of the model of a theory (in physics or in economics) to which we refer. Such a conceptual analysis seems to me to fulfill some of the functions that we can expect from a theory: it defines the essential features of a sub-system; it provides a list of the main variables; it suggests certain hypotheses about the operation of the sub-system, depending on whether it is bipolar or multipolar, homogeneous or heterogeneous.

It has an additional value: it makes it easier to distinguish between theory and ideology or, if you prefer, between pseudo-theories and theories. For example, let us take the formula, sometimes presented as theoretical, according to which states act according to their "national interest." The formula is just as meaningless as that of La Rochefoucauld, who discerned selfishness behind behavior that was apparently the most unselfish. It is enough, indeed, to postulate that Meredith's character Beauchamp, who drowns while trying to save a child, finds more satisfaction in sacrificing his life than in saving it at the expense of someone else's death. Likewise, whatever the diplomacy of a state may be, nothing prevents one from asserting after the fact that it was dictated by considerations of "national interest," as long as "national interest" has not been strictly defined.

Indeed, the so-called theory of "national interest" either suggests an idea as undeniable as it is vague—that each actor thinks first of itself—or else tries to oppose itself to other pseudo-theories, e.g., that the foreign policy of states is dictated by political ideology or moral principles. Each of these pseudo-theories means something only in connection with the other. To say that the Soviet Union conducts its foreign affairs on the basis of its "national interest" means that it is not exclusively guided by ideological considerations, by its ambition to spread Communism. Such a proposition is undeniable, but to conclude from it that the rulers of a non-Communist Russia would have had the same diplomatic policy between 1917 and 1967 is simply absurd. The purpose of the empirical study of international relations consists precisely in determining the historical perceptions that control the behavior of collective actors and the decisions of the rulers of these actors. The theoretical approach we have adopted throws light upon the diversity of the stakes involved in conflicts between collective actors, of the goals that they may have in view. The obsession with "space," characteristic of Japan's and Hitler's ambitions between the two world wars, has disappeared. The Marxist-Leninist ideology of an implacable conflict between the capitalist and socialist camps, which if it has not dictated the day-by-day decisions of the Kremlin leaders, has at least molded their thinking, is in the process of erosion. The Kremlin's diplomacy is being transformed at the same time as their image of the world.

This theory can be presented as a failure or as a limitation of theory. Indeed, if we refer to the pure economics of Walras and Pareto, there can be no "pure theory of international relations" any more than there can be a "pure theory of internal politics" because we cannot endow the actors, either through the centuries or within a given system, with a single aim: the conscious or unconscious desire for a certain maximum gain. Those who presuppose the will to "maximize power" are not even aware of the ambiguity of the term they use.

If we refer to the Keynesian model, the gap between economic theory and the theory of international relations is less wide, but it still exists. There is no equivalent in the international system either for accounting identities (investment = savings) or for the distinction between independent and dependent variables. The international system is even less homeostatic than the system conceived by Keynes: although the latter contains equilibria without full employment, automatic or manipulated mechanisms tend either to re-establish equilibria or to induce alternating movements of expansion and contraction. No international system, whether homogeneous or heterogeneous, bipolar or multipolar, has a mechanism guaranteed to restore equilibrium. Innumerable are the factors, within states or in their relations, that tend to modify the nature of the system or to bring about a shift from one system to another.

Only a halfway affirmative answer can be given to the last question, but this does not condemn our theoretical choice. Systems and social events are *undefined* in the epistemological sense of the term: as they are experienced by their subjects and observed by historians or sociologists, they neither parcel themselves out into neat and definite sub-systems, nor can they be reduced to a small number of variables that could be organized into a body of interconnected propositions. The definition we have adopted allows us to set up such a body, but we could not deduce the systematic murder of millions of Jews by the Nazis as a necessary consequence of any theory. An analysis of the European state system of 1914 helps us understand the unlimited nature of the First World War. Indeed, a hypothesis to the effect that "a conflict between two alliance systems involving an entire international system, whose outcome will determine the hierarchical position of all the principal actors, will naturally tend to be carried on until its conclusion, that is, until the complete victory of one of the two camps" seems probable. But such a hypothesis, assuming that its wording is precise enough for it to be applied to many other cases, should be confirmed by historical studies. Besides, it could have been contradicted if the course of military events had been different in the summer of 1914. For that matter, the decisive factor between 1914 and 1918 seems to have been what I have elsewhere called "the technical surprise."[8] (None of the military high commands had been prepared for a long war and none had foreseen the relentless mobilization, which was the work of civilians on both sides.) On the other hand, the period of revolutionary wars between 1792 and 1815 can be attributed to the ideological factor much more than to other elements of the international situation. Clausewitz wrote that there is a theory of tactics but not of strategy, because the strategist must base his decisions on a particular situation, and each situation presents too many special features for us to be able to substitute deduction from certain generalizations for the intuition, common sense, or intelligence of the military leader. It is not always ignorance but sometimes the very nature of the subject matter that determines the limits of a theory.

On the other hand, from the theoretical definition we have adopted, one cannot deduce all of what I shall call "peaceful commerce between communities," whether it concerns relations between individuals (buyers and sellers belonging to two political entities) or relations between states (scientific, economic, intellectual, tourist, etc.). There is no prohibition against attempting to define international society on the basis of the state of peace instead of the risk of war, or against considering tests of strength and military competition as exceptional situations rather than essential features of international relations. It might be objected that we have confused international and interstate relations and that our definition can at most be applied only to the latter, and even then only during times of crisis. Transnational (or trans-state) society would thus be presented as the true international society, which supranational organizations would progressively regulate, military competition between states gradually losing its virulence and narrowing its scope.

I wish it would be so tomorrow. But considering the long history of complex societies, the theoretical definition I have chosen seems to me to be closer to reality, more in keeping with experience, more instructive, and more productive. Any definition that fails to take account of the basic characteristic of international relations, which is rooted in the legitimation of the resort to force, neglects both a constant factor in civilizations, one that has had tremendous effects on the course of history, and the human meaning of military activity. Statisticians such as Lewis Richardson who count acts of violence or homicide without differentiating between murderers and soldiers provide an opportune reminder that figures in themselves are meaningless. The theoretical definition offered here coincides with actual

---

[8] *The Century of Total War* (Boston: Beacon Press, 1955), Chap. 1.

experience; statesmen, jurists, moralists, philosophers, and military men throughout the ages have perceived the essence of international relations to be just what I see as the starting point for a theory. Perhaps some modernists will condemn me for this. On this matter, I am a traditionalist.

III

The relationships of such a theory to the social context (or, if you prefer, to global society) cannot be the same as those of economic theory (whether of Walras, Pareto, or Keynes) to that same context. To be sure, economists are far from agreeing upon the best way to combine economic and sociological conceptualization. We cannot easily move from a theory of the distribution among factors of production to a theory of the distribution of income. The historical school in Germany and the institutional school in the United States have sought to define, more or less rigorously, the social contexts (an inevitably vague expression) in which actual economic mechanisms come into play. It is easy to assert that war is a factor external to the economic situation. But is the view of the economic system that prompted the leaders of Europe and America to seek budgetary equilibrium in a period of deflation an external factor or not? Are monetary or budgetary decisions external? The present quarrel about the international monetary system and the ability of the United States to have an annual balance-of-payments deficit of one to three billion dollars for eight years without being forced to modify its internal expansionist policy illustrate, if need be, the way in which the economic sub-system impinges in its daily operations on the whole social system, and particularly on the political system. Power relations (which does not mean military force) affect production and trade relations.

The theory of international relations differs from economic theory in that the distinction between internal and external variables, even in the abstract, is impossible. Indeed, the distinctive feature of the behavior of actors in relation to one another is that, in the absence of a tribunal or police force, they are obliged to calculate forces, especially military forces, available in case of war. No actor can rule out the possibility that another is harboring aggressive designs against it. Each must therefore estimate which forces are reliable in view of what Clausewitz called the outcome of credit transactions: payment in cash, the test of strength.[9] This calculation

[9] In the atomic age, "payment in cash" is perhaps no longer war but a crisis. At least it has been so up until now. I have analyzed this transformation in Chap. V of *The Great Debate: Theories of Nuclear Strategy* (Garden City, N.Y.: Doubleday and Co., 1965).

of forces in itself requires a reference to the area controlled by each actor, to its population and economic resources, to its military system or mobilization coefficient, and to the types of weapons available. Military systems and weapons are in turn the expression of political and social systems. Every concrete study of international relations is thus a sociological and historical study, since the calculation of forces refers to number, space, resources, and regimes (military, economic, political, and social); and these elements in turn constitute the stakes involved in conflicts between states. Once again, theoretical analysis itself reveals the limits of pure theory.

I have purposely used two adjectives, *sociological* and *historical*. The first term, *sociological*, can be contrasted, as the case may be, with either *economic*, or *theoretical*, or *historical*. Pareto referred non-logical actions back to sociology, while distinguishing different levels of abstraction or schematization within the area of logical actions, the true goal of economic science. The greater its schematization or simplification, the more theoretical economic science would be. At the same time sociology, the science of non-logical actions, can be contrasted with history because it is searching for general relationships and does not aim, as history does, either to understand peculiarities or to narrate events.

Any concrete study of international relations is sociological, as I see it, in the sense in which Pareto contrasted sociology with economics (i.e., it is not possible to isolate a system of international relations because the actors' conduct, controlled by calculations of force, is determined by economic, political, and social variables). In *Paix et Guerre entre les Nations*, I contrasted sociology with history as the difference between seeking regularities and understanding unique situations. Henry Kissinger considered it paradoxical that I called the part of my book devoted to an analysis of the global system in the thermonuclear age "History." Perhaps I had an ironic intention in choosing that title. I certainly did not imagine that Weber's classical antithesis between sociology and history would seem paradoxical or unintelligible to the readers.

The historian's intention can be defined in four different ways. Either he is interested in the past and not in the present, or he is interested in events rather than in systems, or he narrates history rather than analyzing it, or he sticks to peculiarities rather than generalities. In the end, the first definition seems meaningless to me because the subject we are discussing already belongs to the past at the time we speak about it. The global system, as I described it, had already changed by the time my description was published. It is true that the historian of the present lacks the archives, the perspective that loosens the bonds between the observer and his object of study, and especially the knowledge of the consequences. A history of the present[10] will serve as a document for the historian of the future. Historical science proceeds by the accumulation of knowledge, yet also by a constant reinterpretation of preceding interpretations. From the history of the present written by a contemporary to the history of the same period written in the next century, the amount of reinterpretation will probably be greater than from Mommsen's *History of Rome* to a history of Rome written in the middle of the twentieth century. The difference appears to me as one of degree rather than of kind.

The second definition does not seem to me to be valid either. To be sure, the professional historian, because of his training and his tradition, pays more attention to accidents than the sociologist or the economist. But the present-day historian, who is interested in demographic, economic, or social data, also strives to reconstruct the meaningful wholes that have marked out the course of human development. If indeed the historian is more interested in events than the sociologist, it is to the extent that he relates what happened: he puts events or systems viewed as events into place, into their order of succession, and discerns a meaning imminent in this order, a meaning that would be lost in any other method of reconstruction.

Thus, we arrive at two legitimate definitions. The historian either narrates events or tries to comprehend the uniqueness of a culture, a society, or an international system. Thucydides narrates the events of the Peloponnesian War, but Jacob Burckhardt, who tries to grasp and convey the unique whole of the century of Constantine or of the Italian Renaissance, is also a historian. My analysis of the global system in the thermonuclear age is historical, although it does not narrate events. After seeking generalities or peculiarities, it has a special aim: the extension to the whole globe, for the first time, of a single international system, a system distinguished by its heterogeneity and dominated by the thermonuclear duopoly of the United States and the Soviet Union.

I have wrongly given the impression in *Paix et Guerre entre les Nations* that sociological research did not lead to any result. But that was not my thought. I tried to refute the geographical, demographic, and economic single-cause explanations of peace and war; but taking space, numbers, and resources into account is obviously indispensable to any explanation of international relations, as is a consideration of the character of political regimes or of nations. Furthermore, by refuting the demographic or eco-

---

[10] A history of the cold war is already possible.

nomic "theories" (in the sense of causal explanations) of wars, one makes a positive contribution to knowledge by shedding light on the constant data of international society, and even of human and social nature, which form the structural conditions for hostility. One dissipates the illusions of those who hope to put an end to the reign of wars by modifying a *single* variable (the number of men, the status of property, the political regime). Above all, one gains a deeper understanding of the historical diversity of international systems by discriminating between the variables that have a different meaning in each period and the variables that, at least temporarily, remain unchanged despite technological upheavals (e.g., the concern for autonomy and the desire for power on the part of collective actors who constantly vie with each other for their security, their glory, or their ideas, through alternately violent and non-violent means).

Within an international system that is historically unique there is room to set up models (all analysts of nuclear strategy set them up). There is also room for the equivalent of what Robert K. Merton calls "middle-range theory." The hypotheses we find in the writings of various authors (e.g., that alliances and nuclear weapons are incompatible or, in a more sophisticated form, that the major nuclear powers will refuse to back up their guarantee to those of their allies who insist on having their finger on the nuclear trigger) can be called theoretical. They constitute forecasts that will be confirmed, invalidated, or more likely amended by historical experience.

The theory of nuclear strategy is in certain respects more like economic theory than the general theory of international relations. Indeed, it relies on implicit axioms: that a "rational" Prince will not intentionally unleash a thermonuclear war, or will not even risk thermonuclear war except for a vital stake. The "rational" Prince of nuclear strategy resembles the economic man of game theory more than that of Walras. But it is not possible to make an exact calculation of either the stakes or the risk. The theory of nuclear strategy is nonetheless a theory, albeit restricted to a particular phase of history and a special problem. It could not arise before the weapons whose implications it seeks to explain. It applies to only a single aspect of the conduct of states in our time. Moreover, it takes account of its own limitations: the greater the stability at the higher level of nuclear weapons, the more the danger of escalation diminishes, and the less terrifying are the non-nuclear military conflicts. These hypotheses are theoretical because they do not take the whole reality into account. The United States and the Soviet Union, for many reasons, can either agree to impose *their* peace or clash here and there without fearing mutual destruction. For the time being, they seem to have chosen the first alternative. Rulers of other states are secretly pleased with this: it is good that the concern to avoid a thermonuclear war prevails over other considerations. This concern also dictated the United States' attitude during the simultaneous crises of Hungary and Suez. It could be expressed by the familiar saying: "Injustice is better than the risk of nuclear war."

Can the theorist approve or condemn? Certainly not. We thus arrive at our final antithesis: practice and theory.

IV

Many authors are severely critical of political science or of the science of international relations because it permits neither prediction nor manipulation.[11] A science that is not operational is not a science. Economic science is at least partially operational since it shows statesmen how to tax a definite portion of individual incomes without jeopardizing the growth of production; it teaches them to control economic fluctuations at all costs, and to limit the extent of deflationary and inflationary movements. It seems undeniable to me that, in this sense, political science or the science of international relations is not operational and will perhaps never be so, at least not until the time when politics per se, that is, the rivalry between individuals and the community to determine what is good in itself, will have disappeared.

Let us consider only the field of international relations. There is no lack of partial studies of a purely scientific character, in the strict sense of that term as used in physics or chemistry. How vulnerable are the silos in which nuclear missiles are stored? Given the explosive force of thermonuclear warheads, the average deviation in range, and the "hardness" of the sites, how many missiles are needed on an average to destroy an enemy device? The method of analysis, in such a case, is no different from that used in the natural sciences. The nature of the new weapons has given an unprecedented rigor and technical precision to the traditional calculation of the relations between forces. But these calculations are not yet sufficient to dictate a *scientific strategy*, whether it concerns a single decision (e.g., the "quarantine" of Cuba), or a whole political program (e.g., preventing the proliferation of nuclear weapons and refusing to assist allies anxious to develop their own nuclear industry), or a vision of the desirable international order. The science of international relations (and especially the analysis of the relations between nuclear powers) has had an effect upon the outlook of the Princes (the President of the United States and the men of

[11] Cf. Oscar Morgenstern, *The Question of National Defense* (New York: Random House, 1959).

the Kremlin) by turning strategists into the equivalent of what were called the Prince's counselors in Machiavelli's century. The theory of non-proliferation is not a scientific theory. It is a doctrine for action that coincides almost exactly with the interests of the United States and the Soviet Union, and perhaps with those of all states (which, for the time being, are not sure of this).

During the Cuban crisis, President Kennedy applied one of the lessons suggested by theoretical analysis: since the major danger, in case of a confrontation between two nuclear powers, is a total war that would be disastrous for everyone, wisdom compels the state that wants to impose its will upon the other to act gradually. It is advisable to begin at a lower degree of violence and, through actions that are messages and messages that are actions, to make known one's inflexible determination to go as far and as high as necessary to obtain satisfaction. Thus the duelists allow themselves time to reach a settlement without letting the irreparable take place. The winner—the one who has finally achieved his goal—will not cause his rival to lose face, and will have left the path open for an honorable retreat. He will voluntarily create the illusion of a compromise even though he has won a victory.

On the whole, opinion in the United States, as in the world, approved of the conduct of the crisis, viewing it as the perfect expression of diplomatic skill or of the strategy of the nuclear age. Only a few cynics have stood apart. They have argued that even if President Kennedy had not taken so many precautions to spare the Kremlin leaders' pride, the latter would not have allowed themselves to be provoked. They would have adhered to Lenin's rule of taking two steps forward and one backward, a rule that takes on additional validity in the nuclear age. I am raising the argument of the cynics, not because I accept it myself, but in order to show that, even in such a critical situation, science proposes and the Prince disposes.

Another example will illustrate the limitations of a doctrine based only on the lessons of abstract analysis. Such analysis clearly shows that the more monstrous a total nuclear war is, the less plausible is a threat to unleash it. The doctrine of all or nothing, of massive retaliation, becomes more and more unreasonable and, in the end, ineffectual. The result is that deterrence by nuclear threat requires the existence of conventional forces sufficient to prevent a would-be aggressor from gaining easy victories at small cost, and to give the defender the means of increasing his stakes until the time when the use of nuclear weapons becomes plausible or even inevitable.

Passing from the doctrine of massive retaliation to the doctrine of flexible response is in keepng with the logic of strategic thinking. All countries possessing nuclear weapons will accept the abstract value of this reasoning as soon as they have the means to apply its conclusions, that is, when they will no longer be compelled, consciously or unconsciously, to pretend to be irrational because they lack the resources to adopt another strategy. But the doctrine of flexible response does not necessarily justify America's insistence, since 1961, on increasing NATO's conventional forces, on accumulating stockpiles for battles to be waged for ninety days without resorting to nuclear weapons, and on planning for a "pause" after a few days or a few weeks of combat before using nuclear weapons.

Finally, it remains true, according to abstract reasoning, that the reinforcement of conventional armaments adds to deterrence by giving the potential victim of aggression an additional margin of maneuver. But this freedom of maneuver belongs only to the holder of atomic weapons, i.e., in the West to the United States; moreover, restricting the battle to Europe and to conventional weapons would consequently spare the United States and the Soviet Union the horrors of war. Once this is realized, the objections or suspicions of Europeans, and of the Germans in particular, cannot be attributed solely to a lack of understanding, as American analysts want to believe. Depending on the language used, the interpretation suggested, and the extent of preparation, the accumulation of conventional forces will appear destined either to make the threat of escalation plausible (i.e., to maintain the threat of resorting to nuclear weapons) or to permit prolonged, costly combat on European soil (i.e., to delay, if not eliminate, the threat of resorting to nuclear weapons). In the latter case, the policy fosters European skepticism ("the United States will not sacrifice New York or Boston to save Frankfort, London, or Paris"); in the former, it dispels this skepticism. But if the Prince does not understand the various possible interpretations of his nuclear policy, if he goes too far in one direction, if he does not tailor his preparations to the extent and foreseeable duration of conventional battles, he will upset the alliance he wished to consolidate. That is what has been done since 1961 by American leaders, who started with sound ideas but became the victims of the capital sin of diplomats and strategists: single-mindedness.

The same is true of the doctrine of non-proliferation. Let us assume that the chiefs of state all agree that the avoidance of a nuclear war is their highest objective. Let us further assume that they all believe that the risk of that war increases with the number of states possessing those weapons. It still does not follow that they should rationally adhere to the doctrine of non-proliferation that the Russians and Americans preach and strive to put into practice. This doctrine implies a discrimination between states, with some deemed worthy and others unworthy of holding such weapons. This discrimination may endanger the security of non-nuclear states. At any rate, it subjects them to the status of protectorates, which Princes traditionally have considered incompatible with dignity and sovereignty. Not to have to depend on any protector is a value in itself, even if dependence does not jeopardize security.

Do not misunderstand me: I am not saying that the Russians and Americans are wrong to subscribe to the doctrine of non-proliferation. It is possible that an implicit or explicit agreement between the two major powers is desirable. But I want to show that the doctrine, drawn from a simplified model and presuming that all actors have a single or ultimate goal, has no claim to validity or scientific accuracy. Whether the doctrine is inspired by unselfish motives or by an unconscious desire for power, it appears to be cynical since it tends to sanctify the reign of the two superpowers. In any case, the doctrine conforms to the essential nature of the system of international relations I have analyzed: it endeavors to substitute the rule of the strongest for the still nonexistent tribunal and police force. Far from having modified the asocial nature of international relations, nuclear weapons have given rise to new expressions of that nature: solidarity of interests between ideological enemies, conflict of interests among allies. Because resort to force is still possible at any moment, the two superpowers subordinate their rivalry not to a rule of law but to a common concern for their security.

If we expect a theory of international relations to provide the equivalent of what a knowledge of construction materials provides the builder of bridges, then there is no theory and never will be. What the theory of action is able to offer, here as elsewhere, is an understanding of various ideologies—moralism, legalism, realism, and power politics—through which men and nations think out problems in international relations, establish their goals, or assign themselves duties. The theory of practice, or *praxeology*, differs from these ideologies insofar as it considers them all and determines the full implications of each one. As long as international society remains an asocial society whose law, in serious cases, is left to the interpretation of each actor, and which lacks an authority holding a monopoly of legitimate violence, the theory will be scientifically valid to the very extent that it does not provide the equivalent of what noble-hearted people and lightweight minds expect, that is, a simple ideology guaranteeing morality or efficiency.

This theory, as objective a study as possible of the conditions under which foreign policy develops, is not irrelevant to the morality or efficiency of action. For moralism, if it leads to Max Weber's *Gesinnungsethik,* by failing to take account of the probable or possible consequences of the decisions taken, turns out to be immoral. As for realism, it would be unrealistic if it considered the moral judgments men pass on the conduct of their rulers as negligible, if it disregarded the interest of all actors in maintaining a minimum of legal order in their reciprocal relations, or if it ignored the yearning of humanity, now capable of destroying itself, to reduce interstate violence. The more the theorist of practice bears in mind the multiplicity of aims pursued by actors in the international system, the less he will be a prisoner of an oversimplified representation of *homo diplomaticus,* and the more chance he will have of understanding his allies and enemies by understanding the diversity of perceptions that govern their conduct. The *hic et nunc* decision, about Cuba or Vietnam, can never be dictated by the theorist. Nor will he be able to dictate, with assurance of scientific validity, the strategy that would lead humanity beyond "power politics" toward a monopoly of legitimate violence.

The course of international relations is eminently historical, in all senses of the term: its changes are incessant; its systems are diverse and fragile; it is affected by all economic, technical, and moral transformations; decisions made by one man or several men put millions of men into action and launch irreversible changes, whose consequences are carried out indefinitely; and the actors, citizens or rulers, are forever subjected to apparently contradictory obligations.

It would be unreasonable to decree in advance that modern methods of investigation will not teach us anything we do not already know. Long live computers, the "prisoner's dilemma," and experimental research on the probable results of confidence or suspicion in interpersonal relations. But until machines and technicians instruct statesmen, let us take care not to forget the lessons of experience brought to light by the effort to conceptualize.

Is it a failure or a success for the theory of practice to rediscover the paradoxes of human existence as they have always appeared to philosophers, both ancient and modern, without resolving them? Failure or success, it is a fact that the scientist has not yet been given the means to transform man's historical condition.

V

Perhaps after this itinerary we can again take up that meaning of the concept of theory we put aside: theory and philosophy as one and the same. Not that we have in some way found in conclusion what we decided not to seek at the outset, namely, a philosophical truth of a higher order than scientific knowledge. But the whole approach, which proceeds from the determination of the international system as a specific social system to the prudence of the statesman through the analysis of sociological regularities and historical peculiarities, constitutes the critical or questioning equivalent of a philosophy.

No technique of inquiry, no traditional or modern method, should be accepted or rejected *a priori* so long as the investigator remains aware of the whole into which his individual undertaking is placed or integrated. The different levels of conceptualization—a definition of the asocial society of sovereign states, a theory or pseudo-theory of the demographic or economic causes of wars, models of typical situations between nuclear powers, an enumeration of the main variables of all international systems—are distinguished from each other to suit the needs of clarity. Understanding of a single system—for example, the global system from 1949 to 1960—must take all levels into account; it calls for the simultaneous use of all available instruments. It is not even a paradox to suggest that theory alone makes it possible to incorporate the personal relationship between two men, Khrushchev and Kennedy, into an interpretation of the development of the Cuban crisis of 1962. In the opposite sense, this crisis adds something to our theoretical knowledge, reminding us that the historian has to be a philosopher and the philosopher has to be aware of what we shall never see a second time—at least when the object of knowledge is not only the logic of systems but also the logic of action.

HANS J. MORGENTHAU

Common Sense and Theories of
International Relations

Aristotle found the beginning of philosophic thought in the "méga thaumázein," the "great wonderment" at an unexplained fact that requires explanation. Following the contemporary attempts at developing theories of international relations, I am continuously struck by two such facts: the contrast between the novelty of these attempts and the oldness of international relations, and the contrast between the persistence of these attempts and the consistent experience of failure.

International relations are as old as autonomous political organizations, and the ancient Chinese, Indians, and Greeks have reflected upon them. Yet with the exception of the Indian Kautilya, who developed intricate mathematical models of the balance of power, and of Machiavelli, whose *Prince* is really a theoretical treatise clothed in the traditional garb of advice to the prince on how to acquire and retain power, their reflections were philosophic and moral, not theoretical. Rather than seeking to understand in a theoretical manner what international relations are all about, they tried to learn from philosophy or history, or from a combination of both,

Hans J. Morgenthau is professor of political science and modern history at the University of Chicago, where he is Director of the Center for the Study of American Foreign Policy. He is the author of *Scientific Man vs. Power Politics, Politics Among Nations, In Defense of the National Interest, The Purpose of American Politics,* and *Politics in the Twentieth Century;* and the co-author of *Principles and Problems of International Politics.*

the principles of morally right and, to a lesser degree, of successful political action.

This orientation toward practicality, moral or empirical, has been a distinctive characteristic of all reflections on foreign policy until very recently. In the *Mirror of Princes,* Machiavelli's *Prince,* the political testaments and memoirs of kings and statesmen from Louis XIV to Bismarck, the systematic treatises on diplomacy from Callières and Mably to Cambon and Nicolson—the concern with formulating principles that are to govern the conduct of foreign policy was predominant. What distinguishes the reflections on international relations since Machiavelli from those that preceded them is not their concern for practicality but the intellectual mode with which they endeavored to satisfy that concern. The Greek and medieval mode was predominantly ethical and deductive; that of Machiavelli and of those who followed him was empirical and inductive.

This concern for practical results dominated, in the most explicit fashion and to the detriment of theoretical understanding, reflections on international relations from the end of the Napoleonic Wars to the Second World War. For international relations, this was the age of reform. The dominant interest was less in understanding international relations as they are than in changing them. The purpose of change was to make international peace more secure. Great intellectual energies and ingenuity were spent on developing theories of international law that, if they could be put into practice, would limit the discretion of national governments. During the nineteenth century, disarmament and international arbitration were promoted as the main devices for putting international peace on a more stable foundation; in our century, collective security, peaceful change, and international organization have been added to these devices.

In the aftermath of the Second World War, reflections on international relations entered an entirely new phase. This phase is marked by a number of academic schools of thought—behaviorism, systems analysis, game theory, simulation, and methodology in general—that have one aim in common: the pervasive rationalization of international relations by means of a comprehensive theory. The ultimate purpose is still practical: to increase the reliability of prediction and thereby remove uncertainty from political action. Yet this practicality is different from the traditional one. The latter endeavored to maximize rationality and success through the rational manipulation of the objective factors of international relations; the former attempts to eradicate obstacles to pervasive rationalization that are inherent in the objective character of international relations by overwhelming them with theoretical devices. The new theories, insofar as they are new in more than terminology, are in truth not so much theories as dogmas. They do not so much try to reflect reality as it actually is as to superimpose upon a recalcitrant reality a theoretical scheme that satisfies the desire for thorough rationalization. Their practicality is specious since it substitutes what is desirable for what is possible. The new theories are in truth utopias, differing from the utopias of old only in that they replace the simple and obvious deductions from ethical postulates with a highly complex and sophisticated methodological and terminological apparatus, creating the illusion of empirical demonstration.

This illusion is made plausible by two interconnected devices: a reductionism that deprives international relations of their political content, and quantification. Reductionism has been a necessary and, hence, persistent element of all international utopias from the Middle Ages to the present. For it is only by abstracting from that quality of politics, domestic and international, that resists pervasive rationalization and is responsible for the moral dilemmas, political risks, and intellectual uncertainties inherent in politics, that it is possible to construct a morally and intellectually satisfying theoretical scheme. That distinctive quality of politics is the struggle for power. It is at the root of all that is morally repellent, politically risky, and intellectually unsatisfactory in international relations. It is morally repellent because it violates the basic precept of Judaeo-Christian morality: to treat a man as an end and not as a means. For it is of the very essence of the *animus dominandi* to impose the actor's will upon another man and to make him an instrument of that will. It is politically risky because out of the conflict of opposing desires for power there arises the propensity to violence whose consummation is the physical destruction of the opponent, who resists that consummation with violence of his own. It is theoretically unsatisfactory because power, like love, is a complex psychological relationship that cannot be completely dissolved into a rational theoretical scheme. The theoretician of international relations who approaches his subject matter with respect for its intrinsic nature will find himself frustrated morally, politically, and intellectually; for his aspiration for a pervasively rational theory is hemmed in by the insuperable resistance of the subject matter.

The new theories of international relations have yielded to the temptation to overcome this resistance of the subject matter by disregarding its intrinsic nature. Thus some of these theories have assumed that since power is a difficult concept to deal with, power is not the central concept giving unity to international relations. Others have assumed that power is not the complex and elusive psychological phenomenon it actually is by equating

25

it with military power. Still others—and they have dominated the scene during the last decade—have assumed that politics does not need to be explained in its own terms, that is, in terms of power, but can be reduced to the manifestation of something else more susceptible to pervasive rationalization. That "something else" was found, either explicitly or implicitly, in economics.

The stage for this contemporary reductionism was set by nineteenth-century Marxism and liberalism. Marxism saw in politics an element of the superstructure whose character and development was determined by the underlying economic forces. For liberalism, politics, especially among nations, was a kind of atavism, the "pastime of the aristocracy," about to be replaced by commercial relations beneficial to all. These two intellectual movements arose from, and provided the philosophic underpinning for, the climate of opinion, prevalent in the Western and more particularly the Anglo-Saxon world, that finds the existing international scene morally distasteful and tries to escape it either by reforming it or by making it appear as something different from what it actually is. Woodrow Wilson, trying to abolish the balance of power rather than to understand and manipulate it, is the most eloquent spokesman for that mood.

What characterizes contemporary theories of international relations is the attempt to use the tools of modern economic analysis in a modified form in order to understand international relations. Their mainstay is quantification. The use of terms such as "systems analysis," "feedback," "input," and "output" (to mention only a few common and easily accessible ones), are revealing; for these concepts were first developed by economic theory. Even more revealing is the mode of thought that dominates many of the contemporary theories of international relations. Whether they deal with the strategy of conflict or diplomatic bargaining or nuclear escalation, they visualize international conflict as a special case of social conflict in general (which is correct if one does not neglect the paramount distinctive factor that the parties to international conflict are sovereign nations with a monopoly of organized force), whose paradigm is economic conflict (which, as we shall see, is incorrect). In such a theoretical scheme, nations confront each other not as living historic entities with all their complexities but as rational abstractions, after the model of "economic man," playing games of military and diplomatic chess according to a rational calculus that exists nowhere but in the theoretician's mind.

It is widely recognized by economists that this rationalistic, quantitative approach is of limited applicability even to economics; for even here it neglects psychological forces that interfere with the smooth operation of the rational calculus. Its applicability is established by the nature of the central concept of economics: wealth. Conversely, its inapplicability to politics is established by the nature of the central concept of politics: power. Wealth is a measurable quantity that an individual aspires to, competes or fights for, controls, possesses, or loses. Power is a quality of interpersonal relations that can be experienced, evaluated, guessed at, but that is not susceptible to quantification. What can be quantified are certain elements that go into the making of power, individual or collective, and it is a common error to equate such a quantifiable element of power with power as such. It is certainly possible and necessary to determine how many votes a politician controls, how many divisions or nuclear warheads a government disposes of; but if I want to know how much power this politician or that government has, I must leave the adding machine and the computer for historic and necessarily qualitative judgment.

Modern theorists of international relations are repelled by history; for history is the realm of the accidental, the contingent, the unpredictable. They are instead fascinated by the rational model of the natural sciences, which appear to be free of these blemishes that stand in the way of the thorough rationalization of international relations. I tried to show more than twenty years ago[1] that this model of the natural sciences harks back to a Newtonian universe that the contemporary natural sciences have left far behind. This rational model is a utopia that reflects the desires of theoreticians but not the real physical world, dominated as that world is by the principle of indeterminacy, and predictable as it is, at least as microcosmos, only by way of statistical probability.

I have also tried to show that politics, domestic and international, is susceptible to a radically different kind of understanding from that which is appropriate to the world of nature. When we try to understand international relations, we are dealing, it is true, with men in the aggregate, but with men per se, that is, as spiritual and moral beings, whose actions and reactions can be rationalized and quantitatively understood only on the lowest level of their existence. Thus what the contemporary theories of international relations endeavor to exorcise as deficiencies in view of an ideal, pervasively rational theory is in truth but the ineradicable qualities of the subject matter itself. A theory that does not take them into account transforms itself into a dogma, a kind of metaphysics, regardless in what empirical or mathematical garb it is clothed.

[1] *Scientific Man vs. Power Politics* (Chicago: University of Chicago Press, 1946; Phoenix Books, 1965).

This transformation of theory has also transformed the function that theoretical reflection has traditionally performed for the practice of international politics. It has done so in two different ways. The main practical function that a theory of international relations must perform in our period of history is to confront what governments do, and what governments and peoples think, about international relations with independent prudential judgment and with the truth, however dimly perceived and tenuously approximated. International relations are today one of the major spheres in which prudence and truth are bent to the purposes of power, and in which superstition takes the place of rational knowledge. As William Graham Sumner put it at the beginning of the century: "The amount of superstition is not much changed, but it now attaches to politics, not to religion."

As it was once the task of rational demonstration to show that natural phenomena were not caused by devils, demons, and witches and that one could not master these phenomena by ritualistically exorcising their alleged causes or destroying them in their imagined human form, so a contemporary theory of international relations must put current notions about international relations, such as beliefs in world-wide conspiracies, naturally evil nations, and revolutions at the service of such conspiracies and nations, to the test of empirical verification. The contemporary theories of international relations are irrelevant to that task. They laboriously evade it.

For these beliefs, which serve the psychological needs of the believers rather than the quest for truth, a theory of international relations worthy of the name must substitute the empirical examination of the historic data that may prove or disprove, as the case may be, the assumptions upon which governments act, and the unexamined beliefs by which the man in the street forms his judgments. Thus the dogmatism of the contemporary theories of international relations reveals itself as what has been correctly called a "new scholasticism,"[2] that is, an intellectual exercise, frequently executed with a high degree of acumen and sophistication, that tells us nothing we need to know about the real world.

However, this failure to meet the practical intellectual needs that theoretical reflection on international relations ought to meet and has always met throughout history does not imply that these theories do not perform

[2] Barrington Moore, Jr., "The New Scholasticism and the Study of Politics," *World Politics*, Vol. VI (1953), pp. 122-38.

a practical function. They operate within a social context in which truth, superstition, and different conceptions of ends and means struggle for influence upon thought and action, and they contribute to the outcome of that struggle. It is not by accident that they are lavishly supported by foundations, highly prized by academic institutions, and influential at least at the margins of governmental action. For they perform two important ideological functions, one for themselves, the other for the official doctrines of international relations.

The contemporary theories of international relations provide a respectable protective shield behind which members of the academic community may engage in non-controversial theoretical pursuits. International relations in our period of history are by their very nature controversial. They require decisions concerning the purposes of the nation and affecting its chances for physical survival. By dealing with the subject matter but not with the issues underlying these decisions, a theory can appear to contribute to the rationality of these decisions without actually doing so. This appearance is enhanced if the theory is couched in language and underpinned with charts and equations that are accessible only to a small group of initiated academics. Here is another similarity between certain branches of modern social science and religion: the suggestion of profundity and mysterious knowledge implicit in unintelligibility. It must also be said in passing that esoteric language and method allow the trivial to appear important and sloppy reasoning to take on the appearance of precise demonstration.[3]

Although contemporary theories of international relations are by and large neutral with regard to the great controversies over truth and superstition and different national ends and means, they inevitably tend to support the status quo, that is, the official doctrine. In the never-ending conflict between the official doctrine, on the one hand, and truth and dissident prudential judgment on the other, dissent from the official doctrine is of necessity the "aggressor." It examines critically what is officially held to be true and exposes falsehood where it finds it. Theories that are by their very existence committed to the avoidance of that task probe and expose nothing relevant and thus give by implication the sanction of truth

---

[3] Sometimes one is reminded of Lucky Jim's comment on his work "The Economic Influence of the Developments in Shipbuilding Techniques, 1450 to 1485": "...its niggling mindlessness, its funereal parade of yawn-enforcing fact, the pseudo-light it threw upon non-problems."

and prudence to the official doctrine. Thus contemporary theories of international relations provide a respectable protective shield not only for their practitioners but also for the official doctrine. By saying nothing against it, they imply that there is nothing to be said against it.[4]

---

[4] The theoretical approach to international relations discussed here has been increasingly subjected to critical examination in recent times. See, for example, Christian Bay, "Politics and Pseudopolitics: A Critical Evaluation of Some Behavioral Literature," *American Political Science Review*, Vol. LIX (1965), pp. 39 ff; Hedley Bull, "International Theory: The Case for a Classical Approach," *World Politics*, Vol. XVIII (1966), pp. 361-77; Saul Friedlaender, "Forecasting in International Relations," *Futuribles: Studies in Conjecture*, II, ed. by Bertrand de Jouvenel (Geneva: Droz, 1965); C. W. Harrington, Letter to the Editor, *American Political Science Review*, Vol. LX (1966), p. 998; Robert Strausz-Hupé, Letter to the Editor, *American Political Science Review*, Vol. LX (1966), pp. 1001-04; Frederick L. Schuman, Letter to the Editor, *American Political Science Review*, Vol. LXI (1967), p. 149; Martin Wight, "Why Is There No International Theory?", *Diplomatic Investigations*, ed. by Herbert Butterfield and Martin Wight (Cambridge: Harvard University Press, 1966).

KENNETH N. WALTZ

International Structure, National Force, and the Balance of World Power

Balance of power is the hoariest concept in the field of international relations. Elaborated in a variety of analyses and loaded with different meanings, it has often been praised or condemned, but has seldom been wholly rejected. In a fascinating historical account of balance-of-power concepts, Martin Wight has distinguished nine meanings of the term.[1] For purposes of theoretical analysis a tenth meaning, cast in causal terms, should be added.

Balance-of-power theory assumes that the desire for survival supplies the basic motivation of states, indicates the responses that the constraints of the system encourage, and describes the expected outcome. Beyond the survival motive, the aims of states may be wondrously varied; they may range from the ambition to conquer the world to the desire merely to be left alone. But the minimum responses of states, which are necessary to the dynamics of balance, derive from the condition of national coexistence where no external guarantee of survival exists. Perception of the peril that

[1] Martin Wight, "The Balance of Power," in *Diplomatic Investigations: Essays in the Theory of International Politics*, ed. by Herbert Butterfield and Martin Wight (Cambridge: Harvard University Press, 1966), p. 151.

Kenneth N. Waltz is professor of politics at Brandeis University. He is the author of *Man, the State, and War* and *Foreign Policy and Democratic Politics*.

lies in unbalanced power encourages the behavior required for the maintenance of a balance-of-power system.

Because of the present narrow concentration of awesome power, the question arises whether the affairs of the world can any longer be conducted or understood according to the balance-of-power concept, the main theoretical prop of those traditionally called realists. Even many who share the realist concern with power question its present relevance. They do so for two reasons.

It is, in the first place, widely accepted that balance-of-power politics requires the presence of three or more states. Political thought is so historically conditioned that the balance of power as it is usually defined merely reflects the experience of the modern era. In Europe for a period of three centuries, from the Treaty of Westphalia to the Second World War, five or more great powers sometimes sought to coexist peacefully and at other times competed for mastery. The idea thus became fixed that a balance of power can exist only where the participants approximate the customary number. But something more than habit is involved. Also mixed into ideas about necessary numbers is the notion that flexibility in the alignment of states is a requirement of balance-of-power politics. The existence of only two states at the summit of power precludes the possibility of international maneuver and national realignment as ways of compensating for changes in the strength of either of them. Excessive concentration of power negates the possibility of playing the politics of balance.

Second, war or the threat of war, another essential means of adjustment, is said to be of only limited utility in the nuclear age. In balances of power, of course, more is placed on the scales than mere military force. Military force has, however, served not only as the *ultima ratio* of international politics but indeed as the first and the constant one. To reduce force to being the *ultima ratio* of politics implies, as Ortega y Gasset once noted, "the previous submission of force to methods of reason."[2] Insufficient social cohesion exists among states and the instruments of international control are too weak to relegate power to the status of simply the *ultima ratio*. Power cannot be separated from the purposes of those who possess it; in international politics power has appeared primarily as the power to do harm.[3] To interdict the use of force by the threat of force, to oppose force

---

[2] Quoted in Chalmers Johnson, *Revolutionary Change* (Boston: Little, Brown, 1966), p. 13.

[3] I do not mean to imply that this exhausts the purposes of power. In this essay, however, I cannot analyze other aspects of power either in themselves or in relation to the power to do harm.

with force, to annex territory by force, to influence the policies of other states by the threat or application of force—such uses of force have always been present at least as possibilities in the relations of states. The threat to use military forces and their occasional commitment to battle have helped to regulate the relations of states, and the preponderance of power in the hands of the major states has set them apart from the others. But, it is now often said, nuclear weapons, the "best" weapons of the most power-ful states, are the least usable. At the extreme, some commentators assert that military force has become obsolete. Others, more cautious in their claims, believe that the inflated cost of using military force has seri-ously distorted both the balance between the militarily strong states and the imbalance between the strong and the weak ones. National military power, though not rendered wholly obsolete by nuclear weapons, never-theless must be heavily discounted. The power of the two nuclear giants, it would seem, is then seriously impaired.[4]

A weird picture of the political world is thus drawn. The constraints of balance-of-power politics still operate: each state by its own efforts fends for its rights and seeks to maintain its existence. At the same time, the op-eration of balance-of-power politics is strangely truncated; for one essen-tial means of adjustment is absent, and the operation of the other is severe-ly restricted. In the nineteenth-century liberals' vision of a world without power, force was to be banished internationally by the growing perfection of states and their consequent acceptance of each other as equals in dignity. The liberal utopia has reappeared in odd form. The limitation of power—or in extreme formulations, its abolition—is said to derive from the nuclear armament of some states; for nuclear armament makes at once for gross inequality in the power of states and for substantial equality among all states through the inability of the most powerful to use force effectively. Those who love paradox are understandably enchanted. To examine the ground upon which the supposed paradox rests is one of the main aims of this essay.

---

[4] The point has been made most extensively by Klaus Knorr and most insistently by Stanley Hoffmann. See Knorr, *On the Uses of Military Power in the Nuclear Age* (Princeton: Princeton University Press, 1966). See also Hoffmann, "Obstinate or Ob-solete? The Fate of the Nation-State and the Case of Western Europe," *Daedalus*, Vol. XCV (Summer 1965), especially pp. 897, 907; "Europe's Identity Crisis: Between the Past and America," *Daedalus*, Vol. XCIII (Fall 1964), especially pp. 1287-88; "Nuclear Proliferation and World Politics," in *A World of Nuclear Powers?*, ed. by Alastair Buchan (Englewood Cliffs, N.J.: Prentice-Hall, 1966); and two essays in *The State of War* (New York: Praeger, 1965), "Roulette in the Cellar: Notes on Risk in Interna-tional Relations," especially pp. 140-47, and "Terror in Theory and Practice," espe-cially pp. 233-51.

I

The first reason for believing that balance-of-power politics has ended is easy to deal with, for only its relevance, not its truth, is in question.

If the balance-of-power game is really played hard it eventuates in two participants, whether states or groupings of them. If two groupings of states have hardened or if the relation of major antagonism in the world is simply between two nations, the balance-of-power model no longer applies, according to the conventional definition. This conclusion is reached by placing heavy emphasis on the process of balancing (by realignments of states) rather than on altering power (which may depend on the efforts of each state).[5] In a two-power world, emphasis must shift from the international process of balancing to the prospect of altering power by the internal efforts of each participant.

Admittedly, the old balance-of-power model cannot be applied without modification to a world in which two states far exceed all others in the force at their disposal. Balance-of-power analysis, however, remains highly useful if the observer shifts his perspective from a concentration upon international maneuver as a mode of adjustment to an examination of national power as a means of control and national effort as a way of compensating for incipient disequilibria of power. With this shift in perspective, balance-of-power politics does not disappear; but the meaning of politics changes in a manner that can only be briefly suggested here.

In a world of three or more powers the possibility of making and breaking alliances exists. The substance of balance-of-power politics is found in the diplomacy by which alliances are made, maintained, or disrupted. Flexibility of alignment then makes for rigidity in national strategies: a state's strategy must satisfy its partner lest that partner defect from the alliance. A comparable situation is found where political parties compete for votes by forming and reforming electoral coalitions of different economic, ethnic, religious, and regional groups. The strategies (or policies) of the parties are made so as to attract and hold voters. If it is to be an electoral success, a party's policy cannot simply be the policy that its leaders may think would be best for the country. Policy must at least partly be made for the sake of party management. Similarly in an alliance of approximately equal states, strategy is at least partly made for the sake of the alliance's cohesion. The alliance diplomacy of Europe in the years before World War

---

[5] See, for example, Inis L. Claude, Jr., *Power and International Relations* (New York: Random House, 1962), p. 90; and Morton A. Kaplan, *System and Process in International Politics* (New York: John Wiley & Sons, 1957), p. 22.

I is rich in examples of this. Because the defection or defeat of a major state would have shaken the balance of power, each state was constrained to adjust its strategy and the deployment of its forces to the aims and fears of its partners. This is in sharp contrast to the current situation in NATO, where de Gaulle's disenchantment, for example, can only have mild repercussions. Though concessions to allies will sometimes be made, neither the Soviet Union nor the United States alters its strategy or changes its military dispositions simply to accommodate associated states. Both superpowers can make long-range plans and carry out their policies as best they see fit, for they need not accede to the demands of third parties. That America's strategy is not made for the sake of de Gaulle helps to explain his partial defection.

Disregarding the views of an ally makes sense only if military cooperation is relatively unimportant. This is the case in NATO, which in fact if not in form consists of unilateral guarantees by the United States to its European allies. The United States, with a preponderance of nuclear weapons and as many men in uniform as all of the Western European states combined,[6] may be able to protect her allies; they cannot possibly protect her. Because of the vast differences in the capacities of member states, the approximately equal sharing of burdens found in earlier alliance systems is no longer conceivable. The gross inequality between the two superpowers and the members of their respective alliances makes any realignment of the latter fairly insignificant. The leader's strategy can therefore be flexible. In balance-of-power politics, old style, flexibility of alignment made for rigidity of strategy or the limitation of freedom of decision. In balance-of-power politics, new style, the obverse is true: rigidity of alignment in a two-power world makes for flexibility of strategy or the enlargement of freedom of decision.

Those who discern the demise of balance-of-power politics mistakenly identify the existence of balances of power with a particular mode of adjustment and the political means of effecting it. Balances of power tend to form so long as states desire to maintain their political identities and so long as they must rely on their own devices in striving to do so. With shrinking numbers, political practices and methods will differ; but the number of states required for the existence and perpetuation of balance-of-power politics is simply two or more, not, as is usually averred, some number larger than two.

[6] See "The Text of Address by McNamara to American Society of Newspaper Editors," *The New York Times*, May 19, 1966, p. 11.

II

The reduction in the number of major states calls for a shift in conceptual perspective. Internal effort has replaced external realignment as a means of maintaining an approximate balance of power. But the operation of a balance of power, as previously noted, has entailed the occasional use of national force as a means of international control and adjustment. Great-power status was traditionally conferred on states that could use force most handily. Is the use of force in a nuclear world so severely inhibited that balance-of-power analysis has lost most if not all of its meaning?

Four reasons are usually given in support of an affirmative answer. First, because the nuclear might of one superpower balances that of the other, their effective power is reduced to zero. Their best and most distinctive forces, the nuclear ones, are least usable. In the widely echoed words of John Herz, absolute power equals absolute impotence.[7] Second, the fear of escalation strongly inhibits even the use of conventional forces, especially by the United States or the Soviet Union. Nuclear powers must fear escalation more than other states do, for in any war that rose to the nuclear level they would be primary targets. They may, of course, still choose to commit their armies to battle, but the risks of doing so, as they themselves must realize, are higher than in the past. Third, in the nuclear age enormous military power no longer ensures effective control. The Soviet Union has not been able to control her Asian and European satellites. The United States has found it difficult to use military force for constructive purposes even against weak opponents in Southeast Asia. Political rewards have not been proportionate to the strength of the states that are militarily most powerful. Finally, the weak states of the world, having become politically aware and active, have turned world opinion into a serious restraint upon the use of force, whether in nuclear or conventional form. These four factors, it is argued, work singly and in combination to make the use of force more costly and in general to depreciate its value.

Never have great powers disposed of larger national products, and seldom in peacetime have they spent higher percentages of them on their military forces. The money so lavishly expended purchases more explosive power and more varied ways of delivering it than ever before in history. In terms of world distribution, seldom has military force been more narrowly concentrated. If military force is less useful today, the irony of history will have yet another vivid illustration. Has force indeed so

---

[7] John Herz, *International Politics in the Atomic Age* (New York: Columbia University Press, 1959), pp. 22, 169.

depreciated as to warp and seriously weaken the effects of power in international relations? The above arguments make it seem so; they need to be re-examined. The following analysis of the use of force deals with all four arguments, though not by examining them one by one and in the order in which they are stated.

E. H. Carr long ago identified the error of believing "in the efficacy of an international public opinion," and he illustrated and explained the fallacy at length.[8] To think of world opinion as a restraint upon the military actions of states, one must believe that the strong states of the world—or for that matter the weak ones—would have used more military force and used it more often had they not anticipated their condemnation. Unless in a given instance world opinion can be defined, its source identified, and the mode of its operation discerned, such a view is not plausible. To believe in the efficacy of world opinion is to endow a non-existent agent and an indefinable force with effective restraining power. Not world opinion but national views, shaped into policies and implemented by governments, have accounted for past events in international relations. Changes that would now permit world opinion, whatever that might be, to restrict national policies would have to lie not in the operation of opinion itself but in other changes that have occurred in the world. With "world opinion," as with Adam Smith's "invisible hand," one must ask: What is the reality that the metaphor stands for? It may be that statesmen pay their respects to world opinion because they are already restrained by other considerations.

Are such considerations found, perhaps, in changes that have taken place in the nature and distribution of force itself? If the costs of using military force have lessened its value, then obeisance paid to world opinion is merely a cloak for frustration and a hypocritical show of politeness. That the use of force is unusually costly, however, is a conclusion that rests on a number of errors. One that is commonly committed is to extend to all military force the conclusion that nuclear force is unusable. After listing the changes effected by nuclear weapons, one author, for example, concludes that these changes tend to restrict "the usability and hence the political utility of national military power in various ways."[9] This may represent merely a slip of the pen; if so, it is a telling one. A clearer and more interesting form of the error is found in the argument that the two superpowers, each stalemated by the other's nuclear force, are for important political purposes effectively reduced to the power of middle-range states. The ef-

[8] Edward Hallett Carr, *The Twenty Years' Crisis, 1919-1939*, 2nd ed. (New York: Harper & Row, 1964), p. 140.
[9] Knorr, *On the Uses of Military Power*, p. 87.

fective equality of states apparently emerges from the very condition of their gross inequality. We read, for example, that "the very change in the nature of the mobilizable potential has made its actual use in emergencies by its unhappy owners quite difficult and self-defeating. As a result, nations endowed with infinitely less can behave in a whole range of issues as if the difference in power did not matter." The conclusion is driven home —or, rather, error is compounded—by the argument that the United States thinks in "cataclysmic terms," lives in dread of all-out war, and bases its military calculations on the forces needed for the ultimate but unlikely crisis rather than on what might be needed in the less spectacular cases that are in fact more likely to occur.[10]

Absolute power equals absolute impotence, at least at the highest levels of force represented by the American and Soviet nuclear armories. At lesser levels of violence many states can compete as though they were substantially equal. The best weapons of the United States and the Soviet Union are useless, and the distinctive advantage of those two states is thus negated. But what about American or Soviet nuclear weapons used against minor nuclear states or against those who are entirely without nuclear weapons? Here again, it is claimed, the "best" weapon of the most powerful states turns out to be the least usable. The nation that is equipped to "retaliate massively" is not likely to find the occasion to use its capability. If amputation of an arm were the only remedy available for an infected finger, one would be tempted to hope for the best and leave the ailment untreated. The state that can move effectively only by committing the full power of its military arsenal is likely to forget the threats it has made and acquiesce in a situation formerly described as intolerable. Instruments that cannot be used to deal with small cases—those that are moderately dangerous and damaging—remain idle until the big case arises. But then the use of major force to defend a vital interest would run the grave risk of retaliation. Under such circumstances, the powerful are frustrated by their very strength; and although the weak do not thereby become strong, they are, it is said, nevertheless able to behave as though they were.

Such arguments are often made and have to be taken seriously. In an obvious sense, part of the contention is valid. When great powers are in a stalemate, lesser states acquire an increased freedom of movement. That this phenomenon is now noticeable tells us nothing new about the strength of the weak or the weakness of the strong. Weak states have often found opportunities for maneuver in the interstices of a balance of power. This is,

[10] Hoffmann, "Europe's Identity Crisis," pp. 1279, 1287-88.

however, only part of the story. To maintain both the balance and its by-product requires the continuing efforts of America and Russia. Their instincts for self-preservation call forth such efforts: the objective of both states must be to perpetuate an international stalemate as a minimum basis for the security of each of them—even if this should mean that the two big states do the work while the small ones have the fun. The margins within which the relative strengths of America and Russia may vary without destroying the stalemate are made wide by the existence of second-strike retaliatory forces, but permissible variation is not without limit. In the years of the supposed missile gap in America's disfavor, Khrushchev became unpleasantly frisky, especially over Berlin and Cuba. The usefulness of maintaining American nuclear strength was demonstrated by the unfortunate consequences of its apparent diminution.

Strategic nuclear weapons deter strategic nuclear weapons (though they may also do more than that). Where each state must tend to its own security as best it can, the means adopted by one state must be geared to the efforts of others. The cost of the American nuclear establishment, maintained in peaceful readiness, is functionally comparable to the costs incurred by a government in order to maintain domestic order and provide internal security. Such expenditure is not productive in the sense that spending to build roads is, but it is not unproductive either. Its utility is obvious, and should anyone successfully argue otherwise, the consequences of accepting his argument would quickly demonstrate its falsity. Force is least visible where power is most fully and most adequately present.[11] The better ordered a society and the more competent and respected its government, the less force its policemen are required to employ. Less shooting occurs in present-day Sandusky than did on the western frontier. Similarly in international relations, states supreme in their power have to use force less often. "Non-recourse to force"—as both Eisenhower and Khrushchev seem to have realized—is the doctrine of powerful states. Powerful states need to use force less often than their weaker neighbors because the strong can more often protect their interests or work their wills in other ways—by persuasion and cajolery, by economic bargaining and bribery, by the extension of aid, or finally by posing deterrent threats. Since states with large nuclear armories do not actually "use" them, force is said to be discounted. Such reasoning is fallacious. Possession of power should not be identified with the use of force, and the usefulness of force should not be confused with its usability. To introduce such confusions into the analysis of power is compar-

[11] Cf. Carr, *The Twenty Years' Crisis,* pp. 103, 129-32.

able to saying that the police force that seldom if ever employs violence is weak or that a police force is strong only when policemen are swinging their clubs. To vary the image, it is comparable to saying that a man with large assets is not rich if he spends little money or that a man is rich only if he spends a lot of it.

But the argument, which we should not lose sight of, is that just as the miser's money may grossly depreciate in value over the years, so the great powers' military strength has lost much of its usability. If military force is like currency that cannot even be spent or money that has lost much of its worth, then is not forbearance in its use merely a way of disguising its depreciated value? Conrad von Hötzendorf, Austrian Chief of Staff prior to the First World War, looked upon military power as though it were a capital sum, useless unless invested. In his view, the investment of military force was ultimately its commitment to battle.[12] It may be permissible to reason in this way, but it makes the result of the reasoning a foregone conclusion. As Robert W. Tucker has noted, those who argue that force has lost its utility do so "in terms of its virtually uncontrolled use." But, he adds, "alter the assumption on which the argument proceeds—consider the functions served by military power so long as it is not overtly employed or employed only with restraint—and precisely the opposite conclusion may be drawn."[13]

In the reasoning of Conrad, military force is most useful at the moment of its employment in war. Depending on a country's situation, it may make much better sense to say that military force is most useful when it deters an attack, that is, when it need not be used in battle at all. When the strongest state militarily is also a status-quo power, non-use of force is a sign of its strength. Force is most useful, or best serves the interests of such a state, when it need not be used in the actual conduct of warfare. Again, the reasoning is old-fashioned. Throughout a century that ended in 1914, the British navy was powerful enough to scare off all comers, while Britain carried out occasional imperial ventures in odd parts of the world. Only as

---

[12] "The sums spent for the war power is money wasted," he maintained, " if the war power remains unused for obtaining political advantages. In some cases the mere threat will suffice and the war power thus becomes useful, but others can be obtained only through the warlike use of the war power itself, that is, by war undertaken in time; if this moment is missed, the capital is lost. In this sense, war becomes a great financial enterprise of the State." Quoted in Alfred Vagts, *Defense and Diplomacy: The Soldier and the Conduct of Foreign Relations* (New York: King's Crown Press, 1956), p. 361.

[13] Robert W. Tucker, "Peace and War," *World Politics*, Vol. XVII (Jan. 1965), p. 324 fn. For a comprehensive and profound examination of the use of force internationally, see Robert Osgood and Robert Tucker, *Force, Order, and Justice* (forthcoming).

Britain's power weakened did her military forces have to be used to fight a full-scale war. By being used, her military power had surely become less useful.

Force is cheap, especially for a status-quo power, if its very existence works against its use. What does it mean then to say that the cost of using force has increased while its utility has lessened? It is highly important, indeed useful, to think in "cataclysmic terms," to live in dread of all-out war, and to base military calculations on the forces needed for the ultimate but unlikely crisis. That the United States does so, and that the Soviet Union apparently does too, makes the cataclysm less likely to occur. But not only that. Nuclear weapons deter nuclear weapons; they also serve as a means of limiting escalation. The temptation of one country to employ larger and larger amounts of force is lessened if its opponent has the ability to raise the ante. Conventional force may be used more hesitantly than it would be in the absence of nuclear weapons because it cannot be assumed that escalation will be perfectly regulated. But force can be used with less hesitation by those states able to parry, to thrust, and to threaten at varied levels of military endeavor.

Where power is seen to be balanced, whether or not the balance is nuclear, it may seem that the resultant of opposing forces is zero. But this is misleading. The vectors of national force do not meet at a point, if only because the power of a state does not resolve into a single vector. Military force is divisible, especially for the state that can afford a lot of it. In a nuclear world, contrary to some assertions, the dialectic of inequality does not produce the effective equality of strong and weak states. Lesser states that decide to establish a nuclear arsenal by slighting their conventional forces render themselves unable to meet any threat to themselves other than the ultimate one (and that doubtfully). By way of contrast, the military doctrine of the United States, to which the organization of her forces corresponds, is one of flexible response. Great powers are strong not simply because they have nuclear weapons but also because their immense resources enable them to generate and maintain power of all types, military and other, at different technological levels.

Just as the state that refrains from applying force is said to betray its weakness, so the state that has trouble in exercising control is said to display the defectiveness of its power. In such a conclusion, the elementary error of identifying power with control is evident. Absence of control or failure to press hard to achieve it may indicate either that the would-be controller noticed that, try as he might, he would have insufficient force or inappropriate types of force at his command; or it may indicate that he chose to make less than a maximum effort because imposition of control was not regarded as very important. One student of international relations has remarked that "though the weapons of mass destruction grow more and more ferociously efficient, the revolutionary guerrilla armed with nothing more advanced than an old rifle and a nineteenth-century political doctrine has proved the most effective means yet devised for altering the world power-balance."[14] But the revolutionary guerrilla wins civil wars, not international ones, and no civil war can change the balance of power in the world unless it takes place in the United States or the Soviet Union. Enough of them have occurred since the Second World War to make the truth of this statement clear without need for further analysis. Even in China, the most populous of states, a civil war that led to a change of allegiance in the cold war did not seriously tilt the world balance.

Two states that enjoy wide margins of power over other states need worry little about changes that occur among the latter. Failure to act may then not betray the frustrations of impotence; instead it may demonstrate the serenity of power. The United States, having chosen to intervene in Vietnam, has limited the use of its military force. Because no realignment of national power in Vietnam could in itself affect the balance of power between the United States and the Soviet Union—or even noticeably alter the imbalance of power between the United States and China—the United States need not have intervened at all. Whether or not it could have safely "passed" in Southeast Asia, the American government chose not to do so; nor have its costly, long-sustained efforts brought success. If military power can be equated with control, then the United States has indeed demonstrated its weakness. The case is instructive. The People's Republic of China has not moved militarily against any country of Southeast Asia. The United States could successfully counter such a move, one would expect, by opposing military force with military force. What has worried some people and led others to sharpen their statements about the weakness of the powerful is that the United States, hard though it has tried, has been unable to put down insurrection and halt the possible spread of Communist ideology.

Here again old truths need to be brought into focus. As David Hume long ago noted, "force is always on the side of the governed."[15] The gover-

---

[14] Coral Bell, "Non-Alignment and the Power Balance," *Survival*, Vol. V (Nov.-Dec. 1963), p. 255.

[15] "The soldan of Egypt or the emperor of Rome," he went on to say, "might drive his harmless subjects like brute beasts against their sentiments and inclination. But he must, at least, have led his *mamalukes* or *praetorian bands*, like men, by their opinion." "Of the First Principles of Government," in *Hume's Moral and Political Philosophy*, ed. by Henry D. Aiken (New York: Hafner, 1948), p. 307.

nors, being few in number, depend for the exercise of their rule upon the more or less willing assent of their subjects. If sullen disregard is the response to every command, no government can rule. And if a country, because of internal disorder and lack of coherence, is unable to rule itself, no body of foreigners, whatever the military force at its command, can reasonably hope to do so. If Communism is the threat to Southeast Asia, then military forces are not the right means for countering it. If insurrection is the problem, then it can hardly be hoped that an alien army will be able to pacify a country that is unable to govern itself. Foreign troops, though not irrelevant to such problems, can only be of indirect help. Military force, used internationally, is a means of establishing control over a territory, not of exercising control within it. The threat of a nation to use military force, whether nuclear or conventional, is pre-eminently a means of affecting another state's external behavior, of dissuading a state from launching a career of aggression and of meeting the aggression if dissuasion should fail.

Dissuasion or deterrence is easier to accomplish than "compellence," to use an apt term invented by Thomas C. Schelling.[16] Compellence is more difficult to achieve than deterrence, and its contrivance is a more intricate affair. In Vietnam, the United States faces not merely the task of compelling a particular action but of promoting an effective political order. Those who argue from such a case that force has depreciated in value fail in their analyses to apply their own historical and political knowledge. The master builders of imperial rule, such men as Bugeaud, Galliéni, and Lyautey, played both political and military roles. In like fashion, successful counter-revolutionary efforts have been directed by such men as Templer and Magsaysay, who combined military resources with political instruments.[17] Military forces, whether domestic or foreign, are insufficient for the task of pacification, the more so if a country is rent by faction and if its people are politically engaged and active. To say that militarily strong states are feeble because they cannot easily bring order to minor states is like saying that a pneumatic hammer is weak because it is not suitable for drilling decayed teeth. It is to confuse the purpose of instruments and to confound the means of external power with the agencies of internal governance. Inability to exercise *political* control over others does not indicate *military* weakness. Strong states cannot do everything with their military forces, as Napoleon

---

[16] Thomas C. Schelling, *Arms and Influence* (New Haven: Yale University Press, 1966), pp. 70-71.

[17] The point is well made by Samuel P. Huntington, "Patterns of Violence in World Politics," in *Changing Patterns of Military Politics*, ed. by Samuel P. Huntington (New York: The Free Press of Glencoe, 1962), p. 28.

acutely realized; but they are able to do things that militarily weak states cannot do. The People's Republic of China can no more solve the problems of governance in some Latin American country than the United States can in Southeast Asia. But the United States can intervene with great military force in far quarters of the world while wielding an effective deterrent against escalation. Such action exceeds the capabilities of all but the strongest of states.

Differences in strength do matter, though not for every conceivable purpose. To deduce the weakness of the powerful from this qualifying clause is a misleading use of words. One sees in such a case as Vietnam not the *weakness* of great military power in a nuclear world but instead a clear illustration of the *limits* of military force in the world of the present as always.

III

Only a sketch, intended to be suggestive, can here be offered of the connections between the present structure of the global balance of power, the relations of states, and the use of force internationally.

Unbalanced power is a danger to weak states. It may also be a danger to strong ones. An imbalance of power, by feeding the ambition of some states to extend their control, may tempt them to dangerously adventurous activity. Safety for all states, one may then conclude, depends upon the maintenance of a balance among them. Ideally, in this view, the rough equality of states gives each of them the ability to fend for itself. Equality may then also be viewed as a morally desirable condition. Each of the states within the arena of balance will have at least a modest ability to maintain its integrity. At the same time, inequality violates one's sense of justice and leads to national resentments that are in many ways troublesome. Because inequality is inherent in the state system, however, it cannot be removed. At the pinnacle of power, only a few states coexist as approximate equals; in relation to them, other states are of lesser moment. The bothersome qualities of this inevitable inequality of states should not cause one to overlook its virtues. In an economy, in a polity, or in the world at large, extreme equality is associated with instability. To draw another domestic analogy: where individualism is extreme, where society is atomistic, and where secondary organizations are lacking, government tends either to break down into anarchy or to become highly centralized and despotic. Under conditions of extreme equality, the prospect of oscillation between those two poles was well described by de Tocqueville; it was illustrated by

Hobbes; and its avoidance was earnestly sought by the authors of the *Federalist Papers*. In a collection of equals, any impulse ripples through the whole society. Lack of secondary groups with some cohesion and continuity of commitment, for example, turns elections into auctions with each party in its promises tempted to bid up the others. The presence of social and economic groups, which inevitably will not all be equal, makes for less volatility in society.

Such durable propositions of political theory are lost sight of in the argument, frequently made, that the larger the number of consequential states the more stable the structure of world politics will be.[18] Carried to its logical conclusion, the argument must mean that perfect stability would prevail in a world in which many states exist, all of them approximate equals in power.

The analysis of the present essay leads to a different conclusion. The inequality of states, though not a guarantee of international stability, at least makes stability possible. Within the structure of world politics, the relations of states will be as variable and complex as the movements and patterns of bits of glass within a kaleidoscope. It is not very interesting to ask whether destabilizing events will occur and disruptive relations will form, because the answer must always be yes. More interesting are such questions as these: What is the likely durability of a given political structure, whether international or domestic? How does it affect the relations of states, or of groups and individuals? How do the relations of constituent units and changes within them in turn affect the political structure? Within a state, people use more violence than do governments. In the United States in 1965, 9,814 people were murdered, but only seven were executed.[19] Thus one says (with some exaggeration, since fathers still spank their children) that the state enjoys a monopoly of *legitimate* violence. Too much violence among individuals will jeopardize the political structure. In international relations it is difficult to say that any particular use of violence is illegitimate, but some states have the ability to wield more of it. Because they do, they are able both to moderate others' use of violence and to absorb possibly destabilizing changes that emanate from uses of violence that they do not or cannot control. In the spring of 1966, Secretary McNamara remarked that in the preceding eight years there had been "no less than 164 internationally sig-

[18] By "structure" I mean the pattern according to which power is distributed; by "stability," the perpetuation of that structure without the occurrence of grossly destructive violence.

[19] U.S. Bureau of the Census, *Statistical Abstract of the United States: 1966* (Washington, D.C.: Government Printing Office, 1966), p. 165.

nificant outbreaks of violence. . . ."[20] Of course, not only violence is at issue. To put the point in more general terms, strong structures are able to moderate and absorb destabilizing changes; weak structures succumb to them.

No political structure, whether domestic or international, can guarantee stability. The question that one must ask is not whether a given distribution of power is stable but how stable different distributions of power are likely to be. For a number of reasons, the bipolar world of the past two decades has been highly stable.[21] The two leading states have a common interest in stability: they would at least like to maintain their positions. In one respect, bipolarity is expressed as the reciprocal control of the two strongest states by each other out of their mutual antagonism. What is unpredictable in such a two-party competition is whether one party will try to eliminate the other. Nuclear forces of second-strike capacity induce an added caution. Here again force is useful, and its usefulness is reinforced in proportion as its use is forestalled. Fear of major war induces caution all around; the Soviet Union and the United States wield the means of inducing that caution.

The constraints of duopolistic competition press in one direction: duopolists eye each other warily, and each is very sensitive to the gains of the other. Working in the opposite direction, however, is the existence of the immense difference in power between the two superpowers and the states of middle or lesser rank. This condition of inequality makes it unlikely that any shifts in the alignment of states would very much help or hurt either of the two leading powers. If few changes can damage the vital interests of either of them, then both can be moderate in their responses. Not being dependent upon allies, the United States and the Soviet Union are free to design strategies in accord with their interests. Since the power actually and potentially at the disposal of each of them far exceeds that of their closest competitors, they are able to control in some measure the possibly destabilizing acts of third parties or to absorb their effects. The Americans and Russians, for example, can acquire the means of defending themselves against the nuclear assaults that the Chinese and French may be able to launch by the mid-1970's. Anti-ballistic-missile systems, useful against missiles launched in small number, are themselves anti-proliferation devices. With considerable expectation of success, states with vast economic, scientific, and technological resources can hope to counter the armaments and actions

---

[20] *The New York Times*, May 19, 1966, p. 11.

[21] For further examination of the proposition, see Kenneth N. Waltz, "The Stability of a Bipolar World," *Daedalus*, Vol. XCIII (Summer 1964), pp. 881-909. On the possibility of exercising control, see Waltz, "Contention and Management in International Relations," *World Politics*, Vol. XVII (July 1965), pp. 720-44.

of others and to reduce their destabilizing effects.[22] The extent of the difference in national capabilities makes the bipolar structure resilient. Defection of allies and national shifts of allegiance do not decisively alter the structure. Because they do not, recalcitrant allies may be treated with indifference; they may even be effectively disciplined. Pressure can be applied to moderate the behavior of third states or to check and contain their activities. The Suez venture of Britain and France was stopped by American financial pressure. Chiang Kai-shek has been kept on a leash by denying him the means of invasion. The prospective loss of foreign aid helped to halt warfare between Pakistan and India, as did the Soviet Union's persuasion. In such ways, the wielding of great power can be useful.

The above examples illustrate hierarchical control operating in a way that often goes unnoticed because the means by which control is exercised are not institutionalized. What management there now is in international relations must be provided, singly and occasionally together, by the duopolists at the top. In certain ways, some of them suggested above, the inequality of states in a bipolar world enables the two most powerful states to develop a rich variety of controls and to follow flexible strategies in using them.

A good many statements about the obsolescence of force, the instability of international politics, and the disappearance of the bipolar order are made because no distinction has been clearly and consistently drawn between international structure, on the one hand, and the relations of states on the other. For more than two decades, power has been narrowly concentrated; and force has been used, not orgiastically as in the world wars of this century, but in a controlled way and for conscious political purposes. Power may be present when force is not used, but force is also used openly. A catalogue of examples would be both complex and lengthy. It would contain such items, on the American side of the ledger, as the garrisoning of Berlin, its supply by airlift during the blockade, the stationing of troops in Europe, the establishment of bases in Japan and elsewhere, the waging of war in Korea and Vietnam, and the "quarantine" of Cuba. Seldom if ever has force been more variously, more persistently, and more widely applied; and seldom has it been more consciously used as an instrument of national policy. Since the war we have seen, not the cancellation of force by nuclear stalemate, but instead the political organization and pervasion of power; not the end of balance of power owing to a reduction in the number of major states, but instead the formation and perpetuation of a balance *à deux*.

---

[22] On the limitations of a small nuclear force, see Waltz, *Foreign Policy and Democratic Politics* (Boston: Little, Brown, 1967), pp. 145-48.

KARL W. DEUTSCH

On the Concepts of Politics and Power*

Some Concepts About Politics

Among the vast number of human relations, which ones are *political?*
What does politics do that other human activities and institutions do not
do?

Politics consists of the more or less incomplete control of human behavior through voluntary habits of *compliance* in combination with threats
of probable *enforcement*. In its essence, politics is based on the interplay
of these two things: habits and threats.

The *habits* of behaving, cooperating, obeying the law, or respecting
some decision as binding tend to be voluntary for most people. For habits
are part of our nature and of the way we more or less automatically act.
Without these habits, there could be no law and no government as we
know them. Only because most drivers stick to the right-hand side of the
road and stop at red lights can the traffic code be enforced at a tolerable

* This attempt at a somewhat more unified restatement of certain concepts from re-
cent theories of politics and international relations is a draft for part of a forthcoming
book on *The Analysis of International Relations* (Englewood Cliffs, N.J.: Prentice-
Hall, 1967). Research drawn upon in its preparation was supported in part by the
Carnegie Corporation and by the National Science Foundation through the Yale
Political Data Program.

Karl W. Deutsch is professor of political science at Yale University. He is the author
of *Nationalism and Social Communication, Political Community and the North Atlantic Area, The Nerves of Government, Foreign Policy in World Politics, Modern
Political Systems, World Handbook of Political and Social Indicators,* and *The Integration of Political Communities.* He is the co-author of *Germany Rejoins the Powers.*

cost. Only because most people do not steal cars can the police protect our streets against the few who do. If a law is not obeyed voluntarily and habitually by, say, at least 90 per cent of the people, either it becomes a dead letter, or it becomes very expensive to enforce, or it becomes a noble but unreliable experiment like Prohibition. The voluntary or habitual compliance of the mass of the population is the invisible but very real basis of power for every government.

Although this compliance is largely voluntary, it is not entirely so. If it were, we would be dealing not with politics but with folkways, custom, and morality. In politics, the compliance habits of the many are preserved and reinforced by the *probability of enforcement* against the few who may transgress the law or disobey the government.

Enforcement consists of the threat or the use of rewards or punishments. In practice, punishments are used more often than rewards. Punishments are usually cheaper; some people enjoy applying them under an ideological pretext, such as Communism or anti-Communism; and many people think they are more reliable. Clearly, where most people are in the habit of obeying the law anyhow, it would seem costly and needless to offer them rewards for it; it seems cheaper and more efficient to threaten penalties for the few who disobey. Punishments may deter some transgressors from repeating their offense, but it is more important that they deter others from following their example.

Enforcement usually is not certain; it is only probable. But ordinarily the likelihood of enforcement, together with the compliance habits of most of the population, is enough to keep the proportion of serious transgressions down to a tolerable level. The punishment of nine out of ten murderers might be enough to deter a good share of those who might otherwise commit premeditated murder. And convictions in only one-fourth of the automobile-theft cases might suffice, together with the law-abiding habits of most people, to prevent most automobile thefts.

Even the most certain or most cruel punishments, of course, do not deter those murderers who are too thoughtless, too confident, or too passionately excited to care or think realistically about the chance of getting caught. This fact points up one of the weaknesses of deterrence, whether against murder or war.

The conditions that determine the effectiveness of enforcement are much the same as those that determine the frequency of obedient or law-abiding behavior. Most significant among these are the strength of the compliance habits of the bulk of the people, and their willingness to give active support to the government in upholding its commands and laws. Next in importance are all the other conditions that influence the relative probabilities of law-abiding vs. law-breaking behavior to which the threat of enforcement is being applied. (E.g., if there is hunger among the poor, more people are likely to steal bread.) The size and efficiency of the enforcement apparatus ranks only third in importance. Least important are the processes of changing rules, passing new laws, or threatening more severe punishments.

However, mass habits of compliance and general social conditions, the most powerful long-run influences on the behavior of the population, are the most difficult to manipulate. Even the size, training, equipment, and morale of the enforcement personnel—the armed forces, police, judiciary, and to some extent the civil service—can be changed only slowly and at great cost. The weakest lever of control thus becomes attractive because it is the easiest to use. Passing another law, threatening a more severe penalty, or relaxing the standards of legal justice are much cheaper and quicker, and hence often more attractive than the longer and harder task of effecting more fundamental changes in the situation.

Politics, then, is the interplay of enforcement threats, which can be changed fairly quickly, with the existing loyalties and compliance habits of the population, which are more powerful but harder to change. Through this interplay of habitual compliance and probable enforcement, societies protect and modify their institutions, the allocation and reallocation of their resources, the distribution of values, incentives, and rewards among their population, and the patterns of teamwork in which people cooperate in the production of goods, services, and offspring.

Rule or Dominion. With this concept of politics clearly in mind, we can readily understand the two related concepts of *rule* or *dominion*. By the rule or dominion of a leader, the German sociologist Max Weber meant the chance or probability of his being obeyed. Of two leaders or governments, according to Weber's reasoning, the one more likely to be obeyed by a given population has more dominion over them.

If we carry this reasoning a little further, we recognize what T. W. Adorno once called "the implicit mathematics in Max Weber's thought."[1] A probability, strictly speaking, is a number denoting the frequency, usually expressed as a percentage, with which events of a certain type (in this case acts of obedience to the commands of the ruler) occur within a larger ensemble of events (in this case the general behavior of the population).

[1] T. W. Adorno, "Oral Communication," 15th German Congress of Sociology (Max Weber Centenary), Heidelberg, May 1964.

Weber's concept of rule can therefore be expressed as a number. At least in principle, it can be measured in quantitative terms.

At the same time, we can see the close relationship between Weber's idea of the chance or frequency of acts of obedience and our own concept of the rate of compliance. The latter concept is somewhat broader, in that it includes passively compliant behavior as well as the more positive acts of obedience emphasized by Weber, whenever such behavior significantly influences the outcome of the political process.

Our concept of *habitual* compliance, however, is somewhat narrower than Weber's "chance of being obeyed," excluding as it does acts of submission to the immediate threat of naked force. People obey a gunman in a holdup or a foreign army of occupation so long as they have guns pointed at them. Weber's concept of "rule" or "dominion" covers such cases of obedience under duress. But it should be noted that the obedience is exacted through processes of force, not of politics. They become political only insofar as the obedient behavior continues after the gunman's or the invader's back is turned. Only then, in the interplay of remembered fear and continuing compliance, are we dealing with politics.

When we say that politics is that realm of human affairs where domination and habitual compliance overlap, we are implying that politics, owing to its double nature, is apt to be an area of recurrent tension between centralization and decentralization. For domination or rule usually can be exercised more easily by centralized organizations; threats of enforcement, too, can be manipulated more effectively from a single center. But the dependable habits of large numbers of people can be created rarely, if ever, through a single center of command; nor can they be created quickly. Habits more often develop from a multitude of different experiences repeated over time in many ways. The centralized use of threats or force rarely creates, therefore, a durable community of politically relevant habits; it is much more often such a community of habits that provides the possibilities for the exercise of centralized power.

The Concept of Power

Recognizing the dual nature of politics also helps us to see the limits of the concept of political power. Some brilliant writers have tried to build a theory of politics, and particularly of international relations, largely or entirely upon the notion of power. This is the approach of classical theorists like Machiavelli and Hobbes, as well as of contemporary theorists like Morgenthau and Schuman. The notion of power as the basis of international politics is also widespread in the popular press and even in the foreign services and defense establishments of many countries. What is the element of truth contained in this notion, and what are its limits?

Power, put simply and crudely, is the ability to prevail in conflict and to overcome obstacles. It was in this sense that Lenin, before the Russian Revolution, posed to his followers a key problem of politics with the question, "Who Whom?" Who was to be the master of actions and events, and who was to be their object and victim? In the 1932 depression, a German protest song called up a related image: "We shall be hammers, not anvils," it announced. Who is stronger and who is weaker? Who will get his way and who will have to give in?

Such questions as these, when asked about actual or possible encounters among a limited number of competitors, lead to rank lists, such as the rankings of baseball clubs in the pennant races, of chickens in the pecking order, and of great powers in world politics. The fewer actual encounters that have occurred, of course, the more such rank lists must be built up from hypotheses based upon the past performance and the existing or potential resources of the contestants.

Potential Power, as Inferred from Resources

An example of the relative power potential of two coalitions of nations appears in Table 1.[2] Here the power of the Allied and Axis countries in

TABLE 1.

Combat-Munitions[a] Output of the Main Belligerents, 1938-1943
(percentage of total)

Country	1938	1939	1940	1941	1942	1943
United States	6	4	7	14	30	40
Canada	0	0	0	1	2	2
Britain	6	10	18	19	15	13
U.S.S.R.	27	31	23	24	17	15
TOTAL, United Nations	39	45	48	58	64	70
Germany[b]	46	43	40	31	27	22
Italy	6	4	5	4	3	1
Japan	9	8	7	7	6	7
TOTAL, Axis Countries	61	55	52	42	36	30
GRAND TOTAL	100	100	100	100	100	100

[a] Includes aircraft, army ordnance and signal equipment, naval vessels, and related equipment.
[b] Includes occupied territories.

[2] Klaus E. Knorr, *The War Potential of Nations* (Princeton: Princeton University Press, 1956), p. 34.

World War II is measured, or at least suggested, by the millions of tons of munitions that each side produced each year.

The table reveals that the Axis powers produced far more munitions than the Allies in 1938, 1939, 1940, and 1941, but that their lead diminished in 1942 and was decisively lost in 1943, the year Winston Churchill aptly dubbed "the hinge of fate." After this turning point, the Axis powers fell ever further behind until their collapse in 1945.

Table 2 provides a hypothetical ranking of the power potential of the major nations for the period 1960 to 1963 and projects another one for 1980.[3]

TABLE 2.

Some Hypothetical Rank Orderings of the Power Potential of Major Countries, 1960-63 and 1980

(Based on Energy Production, Steel Output, and Population)

Index Values: U.S. 1960 = 100
Computed from:

Actual Figures for 1960-63 Rank		Projections for 1980	
1. U.S.	100	1. China	250
2. U.S.S.R.	67	2. U.S.	160
3. China	41	3. U.S.S.R.	120
4. German Federal Republic	15	4. Japan	39
5. Japan	14	5. German Federal Republic	25
6. Britain	12	6. Britain	19
7. France	7	7. France	11
TOTAL	256	TOTAL	624

The 1980 estimates are based on projected increases in per-capita steel and energy production and total population in each country. (E.g., for China an annual per-capita steel output of about 400 lbs., or roughly one-half the 1963 level of the U.S.S.R. and of Japan, and a population of about 1,100 million are projected.) No one, of course, can yet be sure whether these projections are realistic. In any case, it seems noteworthy that the power of the strongest single country in both periods is rated at well below one-half of the total power of the first seven countries.

The Weight of Power, as Inferred from Results

Power potential is a rough estimate of the material and human resources available for power. Indirectly, it can be used to infer how successful a

[3] From data in Wilhelm Fucks, *Formeln zur Macht: Prognosen über Vökler, Wirtschaft, Potentiale* (Stuttgart: Deutsche Verlagsanstalt, 1965), figs. 37-38, pp. 129-31.

country should be in a contest of power, if it uses its resources to advantage. Conversely, the *weight* of an actor's power can be inferred from his success at influencing outcomes in the international system.

The weight of an actor's power or influence over some process is the extent to which he can change the probability of its outcome. This can be measured most easily when we are dealing with a repetitive class of similar outcomes, such as votes in the UN General Assembly. Suppose, for instance, that in the Assembly motions supported by the United States pass on the average of three times out of four, or with a probability of 75 per cent, while those motions not supported by the United States pass only 25 per cent of the time. We then might say that U.S. support can shift a motion's chances of success on the average of from 25 to 75 per cent, that is, by 50 percentage points. These 50 percentage points then would be a rough measure of the average weight of U.S. power in the General Assembly. (The measure is a rough one, and it may understate the real influence of the United States, since anticipated U.S. opposition may be enough to discourage many motions from even being proposed.)

Estimating the weight of power is more difficult when we are dealing with a single event. How much power did the dropping of an atom bomb on Hiroshima, for example, exert in terms of its influence on the Japanese decision to surrender? An outstanding expert on Japan, former Ambassador Edwin O. Reischauer, concludes that the bomb shortened the war by only a few days.[4] To make such a judgment, it is necessary to imagine that the unique event—the attack on Hiroshima at a time when Japan was exhausted and seeking a way to surrender—had occurred many times. One would then try to imagine the average outcome for two sets of hypothetical cases: those in which a bomb was dropped, and those in which it was not.

This might seem farfetched, but it is not. Indeed, it is not very different from the reasoning of an engineer trying to determine why a bridge collapsed, or of a physician trying to determine why a patient died. In order to estimate the effect of what was done, and perhaps to estimate what should have been done, we convert the unique event into a member of a repetitive class of similar hypothetical events. We then try to estimate the extent and probability of alternative outcomes in the presence and in the absence, respectively, of the action or condition whose power we wish to gauge. Finally, we infer the power of the actor in the situation from the

---

[4] Edwin O. Reischauer, *The United States and Japan,* rev. ed. (Cambridge: Harvard University Press, 1957), p. 240.

power of the act or the condition he controls. Power considered in this way is much the same thing as causality; and the weight of an actor's power is the same as the weight of those causes of an outcome that are under his control.

Modern governments have greatly increased the weight of their power over their own populations. Taxes are collected, soldiers drafted, laws enforced, and lawbreakers arrested with a much higher probability than in the past. By the same token, the weight of government power in industrially advanced countries usually is much greater than that in the developing nations, although there are wide variations among the latter.

In world politics, on the contrary, the weight of the power of most governments, and particularly of the great powers, has been declining ever since 1945. No government today has as much control over the probable outcome of world affairs as had Great Britain, say, between 1870 and 1935. At present Britain cannot control India, Pakistan, Nigeria, or Rhodesia; the United States cannot control Cuba, and certainly not France; the Soviet Union cannot control Albania, Yugoslavia, or China; and China cannot control Indonesia or Burma.

At a closer look, the weight of power may actually include two different concepts. The first deals with the ability to *reduce* the probability of an outcome *not* desired by an actor. In domestic politics we sometimes speak of "veto groups" that can prevent or make unlikely the passage of some piece of legislation they dislike. In international politics, we find a very considerable veto power of the five permanent members of the UN Security Council formally embodied in the UN Charter. Less formally, we may speak of the power of a government to deny some territory or sphere of influence to some other government or ideological movement. Thus the United States in the 1950's successfully denied South Korea to its North Korean attackers, and it is currently denying much of South Vietnam to the Viet Cong.

It should be easy to see why this is so. The specific outcome that we may wish to prevent may not be very probable in the first place. Suppose that Communist guerrillas in an Asian or African country had roughly one chance in three (33 per cent) of establishing a stable Communist regime. In that case, an anti-Communist intervention carried out with limited power—say with a weight of about 28 per cent—could reduce the guerrillas' chances of success from 33 per cent to only 5 per cent. In other words, the probability of their failure would be 19:1. Outcomes that are already moderately improbable thus can be made highly improbable by the application of a relatively limited amount of power. In such situations, the change in the probabilities of a particular outcome will seem quite drastic. The limited use of power will seem to have changed great uncertainty into near certainty and thus to have produced spectacular results.

The same weight of power produces far less impressive results, however, when it is used to promote an outcome that is fairly improbable in the first place. Suppose we wish to produce a stable constitutional, democratic regime in that strife-torn Asian or African country of our example. With the knowledge that only about one out of every twenty of the developing countries has a stable democratic government, we can estimate that such a venture will have about a 5 per cent chance of success. Thus, applying power with a weight of 28 per cent would still only produce a 33 per cent probability that a democratic regime could be established. We would still be left with a 2:1 chance for its failure.

Even this calculation is far too optimistic. For it has unjustifiably assumed that power to promote one outcome can be transformed without loss into the same amount of power to produce another. We all know very well that this is not true. The power to knock a man down does not give us the power to teach him to play the piano. The power to bomb and burn a village cannot be completely or easily transformed into the power to win the sympathies of its inhabitants, to govern it with their consent, or even less to produce among them the many skills, values, and freely given loyalties that are essential to democratic government.

The more specific a desired positive outcome is, the more alternatives are excluded by it. Hence, it usually is less probable; and, moreover, the application of limited power cannot ordinarily make it highly probable. Limited power is most effective when used negatively to veto or deny some specific outcome. Such a use of power increases the already considerable probability of an entire range of possible alternatives to it, with little or no regard as to which particular alternative happens to materialize.

The power to increase the probability of a specific positive outcome is the power of *goal attainment* and of *control* over one's environment. Like all goal attainment and control, it implies a high degree of self-control on the part of the actor. A charging elephant can smash down a large obstacle, but he cannot thread a needle. Indeed, he cannot make a right-angled turn within a three-foot radius. The greater the brute power, mass, speed, and momentum of the elephant, the harder it is for him to control his own motions, and the less precise his control becomes. Driving offers a similar illustration. The bigger, heavier, faster, and more powerful the car, the harder it is to steer. An attempt to measure its power in terms of its performance would give us, therefore, at least two different ratings: a high one for its power to accelerate and a low one for its power to stop or turn.

Does something similar hold for the power of governments and nations? The larger a country is, the more numerous its population, and the larger the proportion of its population and resources mobilized for the pursuit of some policy (and, we may add, the more intense and unreserved their emotional commitment to that policy), the greater is likely to be its power to overcome any obstacles in its path. But national policies usually require more than surmounting obstacles. Often they aim at specific positive results. They may require, therefore, the pursuit of a constant goal through a sequence of changing tactics, or even the preservation or enhancement of a basic value through a succession of changing goals. The more people and resources have been committed to the earlier tactics, policies, or goals, however, and the more intensely and unreservedly this has been done, the more interests, careers, reputations, and emotions have become committed to the old policy, and the harder it may be for any member of the government, or even for the entire government, to propose a change. Unless substantial and timely precautions are taken, therefore, governments may become prisoners of their past policies and power may become a trap.

This danger tends to grow with the amount of national power and with the breadth and intensity of efforts to increase it. Ordinarily, therefore, the danger of losing self-control is greater for large nations than for small ones, for dictatorships than for democracies, and in wartime—hot or cold—than in peacetime. If this danger is not guarded against, the weight of power in the long run may become self-defeating, self-negating, or self-destructive.

F. H. HINSLEY

The Concept of Sovereignty and the
Relations Between States

Men do not wield or submit to sovereignty. They wield or submit to authority or power. Authority and power are facts as old and ubiquitous as
political society itself; but they have not always enjoyed the support or
suffered the restraints that the theory of sovereignty seeks to construct for
them. Although we speak of it as something concrete that may be lost or
acquired, eroded or increased, sovereignty is not a fact. It is an assumption
about authority—a concept men have applied in certain circumstances to
the political power that they or other men were exercising.

Applied to a body politic, this concept has involved the belief that there
is a final and absolute authority within the society. Applied to the problems that arise in the relations between political societies, its function has
been to express the antithesis of this belief—the principle that internationally, over and above a collection of societies, no supreme authority
exists. Nor need we be surprised at this antithesis. It is a logical consequence of the nature of this concept that in the international context it has
denied the existence of the kind of power which, within the single community, it has been its function to sustain. The idea that there is a sovereign
authority within the single community involves the corollary that this
authority is one among other authorities which are ruling other communities in the same sovereign way.

F. H. Hinsley is a fellow of St. John's College at the University of Cambridge. He is
the author of *Hitler's Strategy*, *Power and the Pursuit of Peace*, and *Sovereignty*. He
has also edited a volume in the *New Cambridge Modern History*.

In practice, however, this logical consequence was not recognized for hundreds of years. Neither the Romans nor their Byzantine successors, both of whom had developed the notion of internal sovereignty, ever applied it in its international sense. It was not until the end of the sixteenth century, when the theory of internal sovereignty was next formulated, that men first grappled with the problem of extending it to the relations between societies. And it was not until the eighteenth century that they finally solved it.

Men had to overcome great obstacles before they could conceive of the world as being composed of separate political communities, a prerequisite for extending the sovereignty concept. Thus, the evolution of Roman legal categories and, in particular, the Roman failure to evolve a true international law leave little doubt that the Roman and Byzantine failure to extend the concept to an international frame was due to the development of Rome from a tribal city directly into a successful conquest empire. The notion of the sovereignty of the emperor in Rome itself was extended to the provinces in harness with the imperial idea, which held that the provinces constituted a single world in which there was only one universal state and ruler, the state and the emperor of Rome. It was for this same basic reason that the concept of sovereignty within the separate community was not recovered until the sixteenth century, a thousand years after this Roman advance had been lost and forgotten except in Byzantium, and that, even after they had developed it in connection with the separate community, men still experienced so much difficulty in applying it to the relations between communities and states.

The drift of much recent writing on sovereignty has been to ignore or deny these early modern delays in an attempt to place the origin of the concept at an ever earlier stage of the Middle Ages. But the argument that even in its internal application this concept was advanced by any medieval mind is misconceived. It overlooks the fact that the sovereignty of authority is but one of several theories that may be proposed to justify or explain authority. More particularly, it overlooks the central feature that distinguishes the concept of sovereign authority from other such theories.

The other theories have been either absolutist justifications of supreme political power or denials that political power can be absolute. Sovereignty has been the "constitutional" justification of absolute political power. Historically, it has been formulated only when the locus of supreme power was in dispute, and applied only as an enforced compromise between those who claimed that it lay with the ruler and those who claimed that it lay with the ruled. It is the justification of absolute authority that can arise and exist only when a final power is considered necessary in a body politic, and only when the body politic and its government are considered necessary to each other.[1] If we bear this in mind, we will recognize that a sovereign theocratic authority—a sovereign pope, for example—is a contradiction in terms. We will also see why the notion of a sovereign king or emperor who is also king or emperor by Divine Right has been a confused compromise, never tenable for long. Finally, we will understand why sovereignty, even in its internal form, was unknown to medieval Europe, not to mention medieval Islam or India.

There was, of course, continuous argument in medieval Europe about *authority*; but the political and social conditions in which it is possible—indeed, in which it is unavoidable—to conceive of authority in terms of sovereignty did not exist. Neither of the universal authorities—the medieval Empire or the Papacy—could be conceived of in such terms because their power, at no time more than a shadow of that which Rome had possessed, was inadequate for the task of making Christendom into a body politic. Indeed, we may say that it was settled as early as the ninth century that, should the idea of sovereignty ever reappear, it would not do so in relation to the universal but nonterritorial community of Christendom, but within the separate political societies of which Europe was already composed. Until the sixteenth century, on the other hand, the idea that Europe nevertheless formed a single community—an idea that was greatly strengthened when, under the pervasive influence of a revealed religion, a pope took his place alongside an emperor and the concepts of Europe and Empire were absorbed by the concept of Christendom—remained sufficiently viable to give great ritual power to the universal authorities and to prevent the development of the notion of sovereignty around these separate territorial rulerships. Moreover, until about the same date—and this further helps to explain why the notion of Christendom, so weak territorially, could become so powerful ritually—the separate territorial communities were under theocratic rule because they were each as unintegrated as the community of Christendom, or the Empire of Europe, as a whole.

Since the idea of sovereignty could evolve only from the association of a cohesive community with a single rulership, these circumstances constituted an insuperable barrier to its emergence. We cannot be too careful about making certain distinctions when we contemplate the centuries during which they prevailed. It was one thing for men to claim, as claim they

[1] For a fuller statement of this argument see F. H. Hinsley, *Sovereignty* (New York: Basic Books, 1966).

did in their quarrels about authority from the twelfth century on, that the separate component state in Christendom was independent even *de jure* of the emperor and the pope. It was quite another thing for them to argue that the independent state had or must have a *sovereign* power within its own community. Indeed, if only because of the segmentary character of that community, no government governed as if it pretended to this latter claim before the government of Tudor England; and no theorist, even in Tudor England, produced a clear formulation of the doctrine of sovereignty until after Bodin had published his *De la République* in 1576. Until then, men could claim that the separate state was *de jure* independent of the emperor and the pope *within its own community* without implying that it was independent of these universal authorities *in its relations with Christendom or with Christendom's other states*. Despite the fact that Christendom was a segmentary, largely ritual community, men still regarded it as a single community of some kind. If only for this reason, this implication was not seen.

On the contrary, if anything is clear about early modern Europe it is this: far from advancing to a statement of the sovereignty of the state in relation to other states before they had formulated the doctrine of sovereignty within the territorial community, men were unable to propound an international version of the doctrine for at least a century after Bodin had made them familiar with it. Even after the end of the sixteenth century, when the growing integration of Europe's separate communities and their states had made the concept of internal sovereignty a viable and even a necessary doctrine, there was a profound intellectual problem to be solved before it could be extended to interstate relations.

The idea that Christendom was a single political society had to be abandoned; but it had to be abandoned in such a way that it was not totally discarded in favor of the claims of the separate state, which was coming to be regarded as possessing internal sovereign power. It was a condition of the discovery of the international version of sovereignty that the notion of Christendom be replaced by a different understanding of international society—by one that was compatible, as the medieval understanding was not, with belief in the sovereignty of the state. For just as the evolution of the theory of sovereignty within the political community demanded some compromise between the ruler's superiority over the law and his continued subjection to ethical premises and political limits imposed by the ruled, so there could be no successful international application of the theory until the notion of the sovereign power of the individual state had been reconciled with the ethical premises and the political needs of an international community consisting of independent states.

We know that this was the problem because on no other supposition can we make sense of the views of those who concerned themselves with the question from the time of Bodin until the eighteenth century. For if it is clear that the problem was a live one from the moment Bodin's work was finished, it is equally clear that until the end of the seventeenth century the bulk of men's writings about it fell into two schools, both of which failed to solve it because they failed to see the need for this reconciliation.

The majority of men, unwilling or unable to discard the medieval notion of Christendom, continued to elaborate medieval ideas. They clung to the medieval understanding of international society as a single society in which the natural divine law imposed a network of common legal rights and duties on the component states. Some of these writers, especially those in clerical circles or in the German imperial area, took this course because of their conservatism. They still argued, as men had long argued, that the separate regional government had come into existence through the corruption of human nature. In their view, either the pope must have direct power over the emperor and the kings or the emperor must retain the *imperium mundi*. Others of this school—men like Leibniz and Fénelon at the end of the seventeenth century, and the peace-planner Saint-Pierre at the beginning of the eighteenth—remained in it for different motives: fear of the increasing anarchism of interstate relations and distrust of the growing Machiavellism and *raison d'état* theories that seemed to be encouraging that anarchism. These motives are understandable, for the second prominent school of thought, a school that included most of the advanced thinkers of the age, took up a position that did nothing to discourage anarchism.

This second school consisted of what have come to be known as the Naturalist and the Positivist positions in international thinking. The Naturalists, led by Pufendorf, held that there could be neither a political *societas gentium* nor any international law—at least any positive international law—between sovereign states in the state of nature, but at most the restraints of a natural, ethical bond. And some of them, like Hobbes, believed that the state of nature was a state of war in which no ethical bond or international law of any kind could exist. At the end of the seventeenth century, the Positivists reversed this attitude toward international law without abandoning the new emphasis on the autonomy of the individual state from which the Naturalists had derived it. They accepted the existence of international law but insisted that the only valid international law was positive law: for them the sole sources of international law were the practices and treaties of sovereign independent states.

We can see now that the main drift of this second and more advanced trend was taking its writers away from a solution of the problem as surely as was the conservatism of the majority of writers. The Naturalist and the Positivist schools of international theory, in their absorption with the new concept of sovereignty within the individual community, discarded almost all belief in the existence of an international community. Indeed, in their insistence that absolute legal authority within the political society must involve the absolute legal liberty of the state within the international society (and thus that what states agreed upon among themselves either could not properly be law or else could alone be law) their views were the equivalent in the international field of those notions of Divine Right absolutism that were currently distorting the internal theory of sovereignty to mean that a ruler who was above the law must also be above moral and political restraint.

We can see this all the more clearly if we now view a third stream of thought in this context. This third school had been initiated by Bodin, who had glimpsed the international consequences of his doctrine of internal sovereignty. Although rejecting the established belief in the inextinguishable unity of Christendom, he held that interstate dealings still required a legal and moral basis. His emphasis on this need was continued by Grotius, who in his *De Jure Belli ac Pacis* (1625) tried to combine the new notion of internal sovereignty with some residue of the medieval acceptance of the existence of an international community. It was along this route and by this reconciliation of old and new ideas that the problem we are discussing would one day be solved. But it was not solved yet. Just as nobody but Grotius understood the international significance of Bodin's thought until the middle of the seventeenth century, so Grotius's own significance was not fully appreciated, even by scholarly and legal writers, until the end of the century. This third stream of thought remained a subordinate stream until then.

One reason for this was the sheer intellectual difficulty of the problem, even for scholars. And the intellectual difficulty was compounded by the primitive international practice of the age. When we turn from the theorists to the practitioners of seventeenth-century statecraft, we cannot fail to notice that they faithfully reflected the two dominant trends in the world of thought. On the one hand, they clung to the medieval framework of Christendom, while on the other they emphasized the independence and sovereign power of the state to an extent that was inimical to the rise of a new international framework in place of decaying Christendom. After the beginning of the sixteenth century, the spectacle presented to us is a contradictory one. The growing integration of the kingdom and its growing resources, including the notion of its internal sovereignty, were being used by an increasing number of states to shatter the medieval basis of empire. But at the same time the revival of empire was ultimately, and perhaps also inexorably, the ambition of every state whose relative power rose above the average.

I say "perhaps also inexorably" because it is more and more apparent to me that it was not until after the end of the seventeenth century, even in Western Europe, that states developed beyond the primitive pattern of international conduct. This pattern prevails whenever the communities in an international system are basically segmentary. Its central feature is the search by each state for physical conflict with others. If a state is successful, the aim of this search does not stop short of consolidating all the communities within range into a single political structure. Although the European states had begun to become individually consolidated and sophisticated before that date in some ways, they did not escape this primitive international structure to any decisive extent before the eighteenth century. There are many indications in the historical record to support this contention. Of all these indications perhaps the most significant—and certainly the only one I can elaborate here—is the fact that it was not until then that even legal theorists succeeded in fitting the doctrine of sovereignty into an international framework. Indeed, they did not arrive at an interpretation of the international system that was fully compatible with that doctrine until the appearance in 1758 of Vattel's book, the *Droit des Gens.*

This was indisputably the first recognizably modern book on international law because it was the first to achieve this feat. Let us by all means emphasize that, like all products of the human mind, it had its antecedents and predecessors. Vattel borrowed from Grotius, whom he greatly admired, a central ingredient of his solution to the problem: the argument that it was necessary to attribute a legal character not only to the positive rules flowing from the will and practice of individual states, but also to the limits and injunctions stemming from the proposition that there existed a natural, if now wholly secularized, international community to which the individual states belonged. He borrowed from more contemporary non-legal writers—men like Montesquieu, Voltaire, and Rousseau—an understanding of this community of states that no longer emphasized either that the states were ritually or even politically a single *societas,* as some had gone on insisting since medieval days, or that they were utterly independent, as the Naturalist and Positivist attack on the medieval view had insisted. What these men were emphasizing after the 1730's was that Europe's states were politically sovereign organizations that had, however, been drawn together by contiguity and historical development into an international system that was a unity *sui generis*. It may be admitted that at least among writers this new conception of Europe had become commonplace by the time Vattel used it as the basis of his international law. Even so, it was Vattel who first compounded the existing elements into a modern statement of international law—a statement that founded the international system, as a system, on the sovereignty of the separate member state.

If one indication of the book's significance is that it is the first such statement that is readily intelligible to a modern reader, another is that it was the first to assume the need for an international law of peace as well as of war. Legal writers before Vattel, not only before the seventeenth century but also after Grotius, had merely sought to civilize conflict—to systematize rules for the conduct of war and the orderly transfer of its spoils. Vattel was equally interested in systematizing the rules that should govern the peacetime relations between states. And this suggests that he was influenced by changing conditions as well as by changing ideas. If it is right to concede that Vattel was able to stand on the shoulders of earlier writers, it also seems likely that he was reflecting the culmination of a major shift in the needs, and thus in the outlooks, of governments. In this connection, it is noteworthy that the *Droit des Gens* was the first book on international law to be used as a handbook by foreign offices. The French government was referring to it in the 1760's. It was venerated by the American government almost from the time of the Revolution as being the guide to "all those principles, laws, and usages which have obtained currency among civilized states." Soon after that, as is clear from their speeches, it had become the reference book for Fox and the younger Pitt. And by the outbreak of the French Revolution it was entering upon its long service in this capacity in most of the foreign offices of Europe, where it was now generally assumed that there was a well-known international law that Vattel had collected and written down.

It may be objected that no earlier compilation could have been used in any case, since organized foreign offices had themselves hardly existed before Vattel's time. The modern foreign office in England, for example, dates back only to the 1780's. But this very fact only goes to show that, if indeed a decisive shift had at last occurred in the behavior of states, it was largely due to the achievement of greater integration and more organized government within Europe's separate communities. It may next be objected that what might be called the victory of Vattel was followed before long by the Napoleonic attempt to return Europe to its older imperial frame. But this does not disprove the proposition that a shift had begun to take place. As with the resettlement of Europe in 1815, when the views of the Russian

Tsar harked back to the federal projects of the sixteenth and seventeenth centuries because he was the ruler of the least developed of the great powers, this merely reminds us, if we need a reminder, that shifts of this order are finally consolidated with even more difficulty in practice than they are achieved in theory. Certainly if we ask which governments first based their policies squarely on an acceptance of the sovereign independence and equality of all states, we must give this reply: the governments of Western Europe, under the leadership of Great Britain, in the struggle against, and in the aftermath of, Napoleon. And if we persist, if we ask when the concept of sovereignty, with all its implications for international relations, became the central concept underlying the international conduct of *all* the states in the European system, the answer must be: only when Castlereagh's ideas had won out over Tsar Alexander's, only when the Congress system had given way to the Concert of Europe in the 1820's.

From that time on, however, so complete was the new concept's triumph that practitioners and theorists alike made the solution of all problems conform to it, as is customary when men have finally adopted a new fundamental idea. In Europe itself governments never again—until Hitler— so misused the concept of sovereignty as to abandon the conviction that they were members of an international community. At the same time, so great was their insistence that every political structure must be a sovereign independent state that they could not settle the international status of the Holy See without resorting to the device of establishing a sovereign Vatican city-state. And when this principle was utterly inapplicable to European circumstances and problems, they could conceive of no solution but the opposite of sovereignty, indeed its conscious negation: the negotiated neutralization of minor communities and of disputed or buffer areas.

Beyond Europe they likewise thought and acted solely within the categories of statehood and sovereignty except when they were overborne by the very extent of the inapplicability of these ideas to the conditions that prevailed there. We cannot fail to be struck by the rigidity of this approach when we see the representative of King William IV advising the natives of New Zealand in the 1830's to form themselves into a state to be called "The United Tribes of New Zealand"; or when we read in a British report on the army of one of the Yoruba tribal states in 1861 that it was necessary to give an account of the "Constitution" of "this Power" before describing its military forces; or when we study the difficulties that followed when European governments, on the assumption that all recognizable political authorities must be sovereign rulers in modern communities, confused the powers of the Tycoon with those of the Mikado, insisted that the admission of the Sultan to the rights and duties of the circle of European great powers would solve the Eastern Question, and made solemn treaties with North American Indian tribes, Eastern potentates, and African tribal leaders. Not a little light is thrown upon the changing character of imperialism after the middle of the nineteenth century by the consideration that it was when the European governments realized that the extra-European areas were not ruled by sovereign states that they felt forced to rectify the omission by the establishment of their own political control there—by the expansion of formal empire. Even the League of Nations could only be established on the basis of the sovereign equality of member states.

We may be tempted to dismiss these attitudes as naïve. But before we do, we should pause to recall that some of them are still with us. Beyond Europe, and beyond the societies that are its overseas offshoots, there are still vast areas that have not developed to the point at which the concept of sovereignty, either nationally or internationally, is relevant to them, but which we persist in regarding as being under the rule of sovereign states. In our views on the relations between advanced communities, on the other hand, we are now naïve in a different way. Having learned that sovereignty is not the sole concept that states need in their relations with each other—a sign of sophistication and progress—we long for the sovereign state to be superseded altogether. And forgetting that sovereignty is only a concept, we seek to supersede the sovereignty of the individual state by superseding the individual state itself. This is as sure a sign of confusion as was the nineteenth-century insistence on applying the concept of sovereignty to areas that were not ready for it. For what would this program accomplish, assuming it could succeed, but the subjection of the most powerful structures the world has ever known to a single authority that would be incapable of controlling them, despite the fact that it would still have to be conceived of as sovereign?

Some may feel that this is a purblind judgment, that these latent dispositions of our day reflect not confusion, but rather a proper determination to replace the concept of sovereignty by a newer one that better fits the facts. To this I can only reply: distinguish between facts and aspirations.

In due course, under the continuous impact of economic and technological change and with the advance of communications, some of the territorial political societies that have made up the international system in modern times may be merged into greater political societies, as earlier the many regional segments of Europe were consolidated into fewer modern states. But we must not delude ourselves by thinking either that this process of reconstitution will obliterate any existing territorial community before the passage of many years, or that it will ever absorb all existing territorial communities under a single state. The facts are otherwise, and our aspirations should be guided accordingly. So long as there remains more than one territorial community, the quality of sovereignty in the individual state will continue to be an essential qualification, in law as in practice, for membership in the international community.

This will continue to be so, if history is any guide, for these reasons: the state is the territorial community's indispensable political mechanism once the community has attained a certain level of integration; the concept of sovereignty is the inescapable justification of the authority of the state in an integrated community; and so long as there is an international system it will be made up of territorial communities. Aside from the unlikely absorption of all the world's communities under one state, there is only one way this chain of consequences could be broken. It would not withstand a universal loosening of the bonds between communities and their states of the kind that set in when the territory of the Roman Empire dissolved into its tribal regions. Under modern conditions, however, we need no more expect the universal onset of this process—as opposed to its appearance in some undeveloped regions where it is only too likely to occur—than the achievement of the universal state. Moreover, its universal onset would be universally deplored.

It is perhaps important to end with a further thought. As I have already implied, to demonstrate that the concept of sovereignty will thus continue to be an essential concept in international relations is not to argue that it must remain the only concept. On the contrary, the question for the future is whether the sovereign community and state will learn to control themselves. To do so they will need the assistance of concepts other than sovereignty. Equally clearly, we can believe that sovereignty will continue to be a viable concept without denying that it will continue to fail to fit all the facts. In an international community increasingly composed of developed and undeveloped individual communities, it will indeed be surprising if it is not subjected to frequent distortion, as it has been in the past. We ought to remember, however, that in politics a working hypothesis is not necessarily outmoded because it fails to fit all the facts, since in politics no working hypothesis can ever do this. And we might even add that the concept of sovereignty will be less strained than any conceivable substitute. If the problem that confronts us is how to make the individual community and state control themselves, it is just as true that, the more they become advanced enough to do this, the more they are likely to think of themselves as sovereign.

ROGER D. MASTERS

The Lockean Tradition in American Foreign Policy*

Few periods in world history have seemed to encompass such extensive
and rapid change as the twentieth century. The pace of events has been stag-
gering, whether judged in terms of specific statistics (such as global population, destructiveness of weapons, or world production of coal and crude
oil)[1] or the broad sweep of international politics (including two world wars,
the rise and fall of Nazism, the emergence, spread, and fission of world
Communism, the invention and diffusion of nuclear weapons, and the dis-
integration of colonial empires).[2]

Among the major new factors in international affairs is, of course, the
rise of the United States to the status of the most powerful state in the world.
Because this comparatively recent role seems to contrast so sharply with
our national traditions, it is of the greatest importance that the character

* An expanded version of this article appears in Professor Master's book *The Nation
Is Burdened* (New York: Knopf, 1967).

[1] See, for example, the exponential curves in Harrison Brown, James Bonner, and
John Weir, *The Next Hundred Years* (New York: Viking, 1963), pp. 50-51, 96-97; and
Bruce M. Russett, *Trends in World Politics* (New York: Macmillan, 1965), pp. 8-13.

[2] Among the many assessments of these changes, the most representative is probably
still John H. Herz, *International Politics in the Atomic Age* (New York: Columbia
University Press, 1959). For a broader perspective, however, see George Liska, *Nations
in Alliance* (Baltimore: Johns Hopkins University Press, 1962).

Roger D. Masters is assistant professor of political science at Yale University. He is the
author of two books to be published in 1967: *The Nation is Burdened* and *The Political Philosophy of Rousseau*. He is also the editor and co-translator of Rousseau's *First
and Second Discourses*.

and origins of current American opinions concerning foreign affairs be more fully understood.

Since the presidential campaign of 1940, Americans have been accustomed to consider the United States as part of "one world" (to use Wendell Willkie's famous phrase); we have become aware that the fate of our own political institutions depends on what happens beyond our shores. This broadening of our perspective has often had a strongly humanitarian tone, doubtless derived in part from our Declaration of Independence: "We hold these truths to be self-evident, that all men are created equal, that they are endowed by their Creator with certain unalienable Rights, that among these are Life, Liberty and the pursuit of Happiness." If all men are essentially equal, the fundamental concern for human rights cannot end at our borders; for some, the logical conclusion is that the United States should orient its foreign policy to the establishment of a better life for all. In the history of Western civilization, several strands of thought have reinforced this image of the equality of all men (and hence the residual or artificial character of the political differences between one nation and another). In ancient Greece and Rome, Stoic philosophers spoke of the sense in which mankind forms a single "commonwealth"; and Christianity radically emphasizes the equality of men in the sight of God. During the Middle Ages, the concept of a "Christian Republic" embracing the entire human race and securing peace on earth was a forceful ideal.

The rise of the modern state, especially in the sixteenth and seventeenth centuries, was in part a reaction against the notions of a universal political community (whose fate had become entwined with the question of the temporal power of the popes); the Protestant Reformation created such deeply divergent interpretations of Christianity that attempts to unify Catholics, Lutherans, and Calvinists led to brutal warfare. As a consequence, it became both tolerable and necessary to admit the autonomy of each state and diversity between states. Since what was legitimate for the French could not be accepted by the English, it was to the rights of Englishmen—not the rights of man—that appeal was usually made in the evolution of English constitutional government during the seventeenth century.

Nowhere was the feeling of political uniqueness more striking than in Puritan New England, for the Plymouth Plantation and later settlements were originally viewed by their members as superior communities based on the true understanding of the divine word. These colonists were so far from believing in the political equality of all human beings that to vote in Massachusetts it was long necessary to be a member of the Congregational Church; as in Calvinist Geneva, the community was bound together by its understanding of Christianity. Since the proper worship of God was considered man's highest duty, religious differences were far more important than the physical or natural similarity between one individual and another.

These historical comments reveal two distinct sources of American thought about man and the status of his political duties. Although the underlying Christian orientation of the West, as well as specifically American traditions, include a belief in the equality of all men in the sight of God, the Protestant and English origins of our colonization emphasize the uniqueness of one's own political community. These two strands of thought persist to the present, as can be seen in the image of an Atlantic community based on shared democratic traditions but separated from Communist states by an insuperable gulf. This may explain why many Americans who are suspicious of agreements with the Communists have also found it hard to tolerate de Gaulle's demands for autonomy within NATO; since the French seem to share our notion of human equality while the Russians have adopted strange and antithetical political principles, national differences should be of minor significance within the West and of overriding importance between any Western society and the Communist world.

Mixing Conservative and Liberal Assumptions

Division of the international arena into "good" and "bad" states is a frequently noted aspect of American political opinions. Again and again congressmen denounce our nominal allies for their failure to support us in Vietnam or their willingness to trade with China or Cuba. According to such "conservative" or "nationalist" attitudes, neutrality in the cold war is a sign of unreliability or treachery; formal allies should demonstrate their sincerity by continued support for specific American commitments throughout the world. In contrast, there is also a more "liberal" outlook in the United States, willing to tolerate divergences with our allies in the name of international cooperation. This more universalistic approach, connected in recent years with the attempt to achieve agreements with the Soviet Union, has been the source of American support for the UN and the ideal of collective security, not to mention economic assistance to the backward nations.

Because these two opinions stem from Western political traditions (and each shares a measure of truth), it should not be surprising that both are commonly held in various combinations by the same individuals. Hence those who condemn our intervention in Asia reflect our nineteenth-century reluctance to be entangled in world politics together with a criticism of the immorality of our use of force; those who insist that we must check "Communist aggression" in Vietnam combine an acceptance of America's role as a global power with an emphasis on the fundamental difference between Western democracy and Marxist principles. To clarify this merger of opposed attitudes, one could say that the "doves" combine the "conservative" assumption that the United States should not intervene in foreign wars with the "liberal" assumption that both the Vietcong and our allies in Saigon have an equal right to hold their political views. In turn, the "hawks" combine the "internationalist" assumption that events elsewhere in the world are a legitimate American concern with the "nationalist" assumption that the distinction between our allies and our enemies is a matter of highest principle that cannot be compromised.

Because most Americans simultaneously hold both "liberal" and "conservative" assumptions (albeit combined in different ways), it would appear that the distinction between "left" and "right" is misleading on most foreign-policy issues. Public understanding of world affairs can therefore be best improved by reconsidering those attitudes shared by all parties (rather than the specific arguments between hawks and doves). More specifically, we must become conscious that some of our most cherished assumptions about international politics are inadequate.

War and Peace

Recently, the dualism of American opinions concerning world politics has produced domestic harmony and agreement in two situations: major wars (where the world-wide challenge to Western traditions also seemed a direct military threat to the United States), and peaceful cooperation with our favored allies (whose goals were consistent with ours and whose regimes have been tolerably democratic). During World War II and in the initiation of Marshall Plan aid to Europe, therefore, the nationalist and humanitarian assumptions of most Americans have coincided, and a bipartisan foreign policy was easily established. Conversely, whenever the question of peace and war or the identity of allies and enemies has been confused, domestic division has necessarily followed.

As has often been noted, Americans are reluctant to go to war, but once committed they fight with a common devotion to the goal of total victory. War and peace seem to be viewed as polar opposites with no intermediary condition; just as nations are either our allies or our enemies, so we are either at war (in which case there is "no substitute for victory," to use General MacArthur's phrase) or at peace. In peacetime, moreover, we tend to assume that our differences with foreign nations can be resolved amicably by the process of "reasonable" negotiations, and that our sincerity will be reciprocated by others. This attitude can, like many others, be traced to our Declaration of Independence from the British: "We must, therefore . . . hold them, as we hold the rest of mankind, Enemies in War, in Peace Friends."

However reasonable a sharp distinction between war and peace may appear, the post-World-War-II situation has not conformed to our traditional image; the term "cold war" connotes a situation of formal peace between more or less declared enemies. The most profound foreign-policy debates of the last twenty years—the demands to settle the Korean War after it degenerated into a military stalemate and the furor over our commitment in Vietnam—reflect frustration with our participation in wars that are not total. Because domestic life continued on a more or less peacetime basis during both the Korean and Vietnamese wars, there were widespread cries that we either defeat the enemy completely or stop fighting.

Behind this ambivalence lies the hope that military victory will restore the peace and teach the aggressors that violence is not a permissible means of achieving political goals. Successful wars—even limited wars—are thus perceived as a means of returning to a peaceful situation in which reasonable negotiations will solve outstanding international problems. This view is shared by those who seek a negotiated settlement and those who demand military victory, with the difference that the former consider reasonable negotiation possible and necessary before the enemy has been defeated. Hence, both hawks and doves share the assumption that a peaceful world is intrinsically different from a condition of war; the fundamental debate revolves around the possibility of military victory and the desirability of assuming that our enemies will accept an honorable settlement.

It is at this level that American attitudes concerning foreign affairs are open to the strongest objection. As long as the sovereignty of a world government is not universally accepted, the setting of international relations will be an ambiguous and tense state of neither perpetual war nor assured peace. Our allies will insist on defending their national interests, often using arguments that (like those of General de Gaulle) seem "unreasonable" to most Americans; our enemies will resort to diplomatic and political as well as military maneuvers that show warlike hostility even in periods of nominal peace. Negotiated settlements will be reached only to be violated by our rivals; and, in our own self-interest, we will be forced to violate such agreements ourselves.

Since true peace is a characteristic of the political life within an organized and stable society, the relations between states are never totally devoid of the basic hostility that finds its purest expression in war. A peace treaty does not convert former enemies into friends—unless, as with Western Germany after World War II, there are compelling reasons of national interest that make alliance mutually desirable. War is not a fundamental distortion of the natural relationship between independent societies, for no government can ignore the potential threat to its interests from states that have different ideologies or goals. As long as no world government exists so that treaties can be enforced like domestic laws and contracts, international politics will remain a condition of potential war and insecure peace.[3]

The cold war therefore reflects the essential character of international politics rather than an unusual situation. Because public opinion could conceivably tolerate the realities of power, it is necessary to explain American frustration with our inability to secure total military victory or with the apparently unreasonable refusal of other nations to abide by their agreements. Why do our political traditions lead us to expect that all mankind will be "enemies in war, in peace friends"? Why is it that Americans persistently hope that victory in war can make the world "safe for democracy," ushering in periods of peace during which international disputes can be resolved on the basis of mutual respect, sincerity, and understanding?

Locke's Conception of War and Peace

Scholars generally agree that the philosopher whose understanding of politics most influenced our Founding Fathers and has remained most characteristic of our political opinions was John Locke. Because the American colonies were absolved, by historical accident, from the need to overthrow a previously established feudal order, Locke's notions of private property and limited government have been uniquely effective in the United States; Marxism has never been more than a minor sect among us, whereas it has been and remains a widespread popular movement in most of continental Europe.[4] To gain perspective on our own attitudes, therefore, let us consider briefly Locke's political ideas and the reasons for their persisting vitality in our society.

---

[3] See especially Kenneth N. Waltz, *Man, the State and War* (New York: Columbia University Press, 1959); Stanley Hoffmann, *The State of War* (New York: Praeger, 1965); and Roger D. Masters, "World Politics as a Primitive Political System," *World Politics*, XVI (July 1964), pp. 595-619.

[4] See especially Louis Hartz, *The Liberal Tradition in America* (New York: Harcourt, Brace, 1955). For example, Hartz summarizes the striking impotence of socialist movements in the United States as follows: "A society which begins with Locke, and thus transforms him, stays with Locke, by virtue of an absolute and irrational attachment it develops for him, and becomes as indifferent to the challenge of socialism in the later era as it was unfamiliar with the heritage of feudalism in the earlier one." P. 6.

Without attempting an exhaustive analysis of Locke, several aspects of his thought are relevant.[5] First, Locke argued that all men are by nature equal and free; from this natural freedom and equality flows the natural right of every man to preserve himself as he sees fit. For Locke, this meant that all men have a natural right not only to "life" and "liberty," but also to property; without the right to property in money and material objects, civilized man's right to life and liberty is essentially meaningless (since he would then depend on the good will of others for his survival).

Locke set forth principles for the kind of society that would most completely protect man's natural rights and secure his property. He did this by emphasizing the importance of the consent of the governed in any decent civil society: if a government can tax or confiscate private property without the consent of a popularly elected legislature, the citizen can be at the mercy of his rulers. But since all men have a natural right to be free and to acquire property, a government that violates the rights of its citizens need no longer be obeyed. In the words of the Declaration of Independence, "to secure these rights, Governments are instituted among Men, deriving their just powers from the consent of the governed .... whenever any Form of Government becomes destructive of these ends, it is the Right of the People to alter or abolish it, and to institute new Government. . . ."

It is not hard to see why the principles of Locke were particularly appealing to the colonists in 1776. "No taxation without representation" follows directly from Locke's theory; since the colonists had been taxed without representation in one way or another, they appealed increasingly to their rights as men—not their rights as Englishmen. But we should never forget that most of those who signed the Declaration of Independence were born English subjects. Locke, the English theorist who defended the Glorious Revolution of 1688, was a fitting source for the principles of the American Revolution because he was an Englishman whose writings justified a break with England.

One aspect of John Locke's political thought is of particular importance in explaining American attitudes toward domestic and foreign politics. Locke's notion of man's natural rights is based on the situation that exists wherever there is no established government; he calls this condition the "state of nature," adding:

> But though this be a state of liberty, yet it is not a state of licence. . . .
> The state of nature has a law of nature to govern it which obliges every

[5] The following pages will focus on Locke's *Second Treatise of Civil Government*, his best-known political work. Appropriately enough, many editions are currently available.

one; and reason, which is that law, teaches all mankind who will but consult it that, being all equal and independent, no one ought to harm
another in his life, health, liberty, or possessions.[6]

The claim to man's natural rights must therefore be consistent with the law
of nature—or, as Locke describes it elsewhere, the law of reason. As long
as men are reasonable, therefore, the state of nature, in which men live without a common goverment, can be peaceful.

This conception is especially important because Locke explicitly describes
international politics as a state of nature. Since the government of each
society is sovereign and does not recognize a higher authority or world ruler,
the relationship between states can be peaceful, just as the state of nature
among individuals can be peaceful, as long as all participants are reasonable in claiming their natural rights. But since there is no common government in the state of nature, each individual or government judges for itself
whether its claims are in fact just; as a result, the state of nature can easily
become a state of war whenever the laws of nature (or reason) do not produce mutual agreement.

Locke therefore distinguishes between war and peace in much the way
that has been described in contemporary American opinions; even without a government that would impartially enforce the laws, peace is possible
(though not assured) as long as men are reasonable. War and peace are
fundamentally different precisely because in warfare there is an attempt to
secure one's rights by force and violence, whereas peace is a condition of
natural harmony between those who recognize the same principles of justice.[7] Although the peaceful state of nature can easily become a state of war
as long as there is no common government, this "inconvenience" does not
contradict the underlying difference between the two situations.

American attitudes about foreign policy not only echo Locke's notion of
peace as a relationship between reasonable men, to be contrasted with war;
they also reflect his view of how to prevent a peaceful state of nature from
degenerating into a state of war. On the level of individuals, Locke argues

[6] Locke, *Second Treatise*, Ch. II, par. 6.
[7] "And here we have the plain difference between the state of nature and the state of
war which, however some men have confounded, are as far distant as a state of peace,
good will, mutual assistance, and preservation, and a state of enmity, malice, violence,
and mutual destruction are one from another. Men living together according to reason,
without a common superior on earth with authority to judge between them, is properly
the state of nature. But force, or a declared design of force, upon the person of another,
where there is no common superior on earth to appeal to for relief, is the state of war."
Ibid., Ch. III, par. 19.

that men avoid the "inconvenience" of the state of nature by forming a social contract and establishing a government. In this way, man's freedom and his natural right to property are protected by political institutions that can punish domestic violence and enforce contracts between individuals. If applied to the relations between states, this theory implies that peace and security are only possible if international organizations like the UN are empowered to enforce treaties and resolve conflicts.

Ever since becoming a world power, the United States has placed more faith in international organizations than have other nations; from Woodrow Wilson's eloquent pleas in favor of the League of Nations to the establishment of the UN, this theme has been prominent in American foreign policy. Why then did we fail to join the League? Simply because it was felt that the United States could be secure in isolation—that is, that we did not have to play a central role in the international arena. Just as Locke argued that the state of nature could be peaceful as long as there were but few men who had little contact with each other, those who rejected American membership in the League of Nations believed that our security was assured by the Atlantic and Pacific Oceans.

Before World War II, isolationism seemed not merely feasible but reasonable; after World War II, an international organization that would secure the peace through collective security seemed equally necessary and desirable. We have therefore oscillated between the extremes of assuming that we could simply ignore conflicts between other nations and of thinking that only through an impartial UN could we prevent a global holocaust—extremes that represent a transference of Locke's principles concerning domestic politics into the area of international politics.

But although Locke describes the relationship between sovereign states as a state of nature, he does not consider international politics and the state of nature between individuals to be identical in all respects. Although the individual can escape the "inconveniences" of the state of nature by forming civil societies, Locke does not propose world government as a similar solution in international politics. Each "whole community is one body in the state of nature in respect of all other states or persons out of its community"; as a consequence, the international state of nature constantly threatens to become a state of war.[8] Since the relations between states are not naturally pacific, like the original state of nature among individuals,

---

[8] *Ibid.*, Ch. XII, par. 145. Some commentators have argued that, for Locke, the international state of nature is essentially a perpetual state of war (like the war of all that Hobbes described as the natural condition of man). See Richard Cox, *Locke on War and Peace* (Oxford: Clarendon Press, 1960).

Locke's philosophy is completely consistent with a balance-of-power approach to world politics.

It was for this reason that Locke excludes foreign affairs from his general principle that actions of the executive should be subordinate to laws reflecting the consent of the governed; in contrast to domestic affairs, where the populace can judge adequately and must be represented through the legislature, Locke treats foreign policy as the "Federative Power," normally exercised by the executive without subordination to previously enacted law.[9]

American political traditions have therefore diverged from Lockean principles in assuming that foreign policies, like domestic ones, should reflect a popular consensus. Locke asserts that "it is almost impracticable . . . that the executive and federative power should be placed in persons that might act separately, whereby the force of the public would be under different commands, which would be apt some time or other to cause disorder and ruin." The American doctrine of separation of powers partly contradicts this advice, requiring the "advice and consent" of the Senate on matters that Locke viewed as best managed according to the prudence of the executive.[10]

This divergence from Lockean principles may help explain why Americans have tended to apply his teaching concerning the state of nature between individuals to the international sphere. Since our legislature must give final approval to fundamental orientations in foreign policy, domestic and international affairs are subject to the same institutional division of powers in the American constitutional system; because the relevant institutions are similar, the problems must somehow be similar. As a result, our traditions have viewed world politics as an essentially peaceful state of nature; where Locke could accept considerations of the balance of power as necessary to any prudent foreign policy (because the state of nature between sovereign states is implicitly also a state of war), Americans have rejected the notion of a balance of power because they view war as an abnormal disturbance in the naturally peaceful relations among states.

[9] ". . . the power of war and peace, leagues and alliances, and all the transactions with all persons and communities without the commonwealth . . . may be called 'federative.' . . . And though this federative power in the well management of it be of great moment to the commonwealth, yet it is much less capable to be directed by antecedent, standing, positive laws than the executive, and so must necessarily be left to the prudence and wisdom of those whose hands it is in to be managed for the public good." Locke, *Second Treatise*, Ch. XII, par. 146-7.

[10] *Ibid.*, par. 148. On the powers of the American President in foreign affairs and the extent to which his authority is less than that of the English King in the seventeenth and eighteenth centuries (obviously Locke's model), see *The Federalist Papers*, No. 69.

Lockean Principles and American Experience

If, as has been argued, this distinction between war and peace is unrealistic, our reliance on international organization is as misleading as our prior faith in security through isolation. Why, then, have Locke's principles—and particularly his principles concerning the origin of a civil society among individuals—had such a persistent hold on American minds as a guide to foreign policy? Of the many answers that might be given, one stands out: as if by fate, America's national experience has closely paralleled Locke's doctrines of the state of nature and the state of war.

The relationship between the original colonists and the American Indians could easily be conceived of in later years in terms of Locke's principles. Whenever the Indians were "reasonable"—and especially if they signed and abided by treaties with the colonists—the virgin continent appeared to be a factual example of Locke's peaceful state of nature. When the Indians were hostile, this state of nature had the "inconvenience" of degenerating into a temporary state of war. As in Locke's principles, no government existed to arbitrate the differences between the Indians and the colonists; as a consequence, the original settlers could only have recourse to arms.

By the time of the Constitutional Convention of 1787, therefore, it was no accident that Americans used Locke's doctrine of the state of nature to describe the relations between sovereign states. For evidence that this was the case, one need only consult Madison's notes of the debates at the Constitutional Convention; as Luther Martin put it, explicitly citing Locke (and other political thinkers), "the States like individuals were in a State of nature equally sovereign and free."[11]

The use of violence to deprive the American Indians of lands became increasingly necessary as the United States expanded inland. Although it could be justified in terms of the cultural and religious superiority of our growing country, the expropriation of Indian lands fits perfectly into Locke's doctrine that property is only truly acquired by labor within a civil society governed by law. The belief in man's natural right to gain posses-

---

[11] Madison's notes are available in *The Federal Convention and the Formation of the Union of the American States,* ed. by Winton U. Solberg (New York: Liberal Arts Press, 1958), p. 180. Others referring to the concept of the state of nature included James Wilson (p. 118) and Alexander Hamilton (p. 158). Indeed, at the Convention the issue was not whether the state of nature was an adequate concept for describing international relations; rather debate concerned the sovereignty of the thirteen states of the Confederation and whether or not they had been placed in a state of nature *with each other* by the Declaration of Independence.

sion of land that is still unclaimed in the state of nature thus gave free play to the self-reliant and pragmatic spirit of the settlers as they moved westward.

This principle clarifies the connection between the underlying beliefs of Americans and their practical ability to solve problems. The national spirit of our people is not, as is sometimes asserted, based solely on a moralistic attitude toward internal or external political issues. On the contrary, within the framework of an unquestioned belief in the natural virtue of individualism, hard work, and the sanctity of private property, Americans customarily approach specific obstacles without many of the preconceptions that long characterized continental Europe. In a sense, the rise of the United States to its present power is a revealing consequence of the hardy pragmatism of our people; although the Industrial Revolution originated in Great Britain, it has reached its flowering on our shores in no small part owing to that famed "American ingenuity."

In foreign policy, the counterpart of our pragmatic approach in domestic affairs has been a tough use of power based on the immediate needs of each situation. Eschewing theories of the balance of power, we have shied away from long-range planning and approached problems one by one; in crises, American power has been committed with a practicality and vigor that permitted us to win every war in which we were involved (at least up to 1950).

The dispossession of the American Indians, who were ultimately "contained" on limited reservations, is a model we have followed in subsequent external policies. When treaties could be made, we were willing to purchase lands and allow them to move farther west in peace; in that event the state of nature remained peaceful and reasonable. When the Indians refused and fought, we sent cavalry and infantry to defeat them and insure the security of our settlements. But in most cases our actions were a direct response to specific crises or threats rather than a settled long-range policy implemented by a central bureaucracy.

Our national experience in the nineteenth century merely repeated and confirmed this combination of short-range pragmatism and the view of international affairs as a Lockean state of nature. Westward expansion was the result of a series of distinct actions, some by those who sought to increase our national power, others in order to extend the territories open to slaves, others as a means of weakening the domestic control exercised by the Eastern seaboard. Whatever the reasons, when opportunities for acquiring new territories appeared, they were eagerly seized.

The pragmatic aspects of our movement across the North American continent did not exclude a sense of mission.[12] But in pursuing such long-range plans—which, characteristically enough, were not universally shared— American statesmen and politicians have from the beginning based specific policies on a straightforward calculation of the play of selfish interests and the art of the possible. We have sought to achieve our immediate objectives by persuasion and money where possible and by force where necessary, being careful to use the threat of our power to reinforce the persuasion. For example, when Spain seemed reluctant to cede Florida, Jefferson confidently stated: "If we push them strongly with one hand, holding out a price in the other, we shall certainly obtain the Floridas, and all in good time."[13] Much the same methods were evident in the annexation of Texas in 1845, leading as it did to the Mexican War of 1846-48.

These events are in many ways characteristic of American experience in foreign affairs. Annexation of Texas and war with Mexico were most strongly favored by slave-holding Southerners and opposed by Northerners who feared any further extension of slavery; attitudes to our use of force were largely determined by the varying practical interests within the country rather than by concerns for the global balance of power or long-range planning. Once determined upon, our policy was frankly backed up by military intervention, though with a willingness to settle outstanding issues amicably; having demonstrated that we could force Mexico to cede the territories of New Mexico and California in 1848, we rounded out our borders by negotiating the Gadsden Purchase of 1853.

Hotly debated, these actions had implications that were not always clearly perceived at the time. The same could be said of the Spanish-American War of 1898, which led to our almost unexpected acquisition of the Philippines and Hawaii (thereby making the United States a power in the Pacific). Our reaction to the supposed brutality of Spanish repression in Cuba, transformed into a nationalist outrage with the sinking of the battleship *Maine,* was based on the same spirit as our attitude toward the American Indians and the Mexican government. In each case, the peaceful state of nature, in which acquisitive Americans had a natural right to increase their possessions and power, was disturbed by an opponent who did not behave "reasonably"; each time, we felt culturally superior to the enemy and responded to his opposition by a frank resort to force.

---

[12] Hence, at the Constitutional Convention of 1787, some delegates spoke of the inevitability and desirability of expansion over the "new extensive Country" in which Americans found themselves. See Solberg, *The Federal Convention,* especially pp. 169, 205, and 293-96.

[13] Quoted in William Miller, *A History of the United States* (New York: Dell, 1958), p. 162.

The impulse to "send the marines" was thus hardly an invention of Theodore Roosevelt. The combination of Locke's political principles and our national experience has conspired to produce a strong confidence in the successful use of our power in foreign affairs. Where possible, peace is preferable because American initiative grants us sufficient control over our neighbors through commercial superiority; when the interests of American business are checked in such a way as to create an apparent threat, military force can be used (as it was against the Barbary pirates at the beginning of the nineteenth century and against Spain at the end of it).

It must be added, however, that the success of this national experience depended upon a global balance of power of which most Americans were simply unconscious. Prior to World War I, the Atlantic and Pacific tended to guarantee American security, though only after we had successfully defended the principle of the freedom of the seas in the War of 1812 and declared our intention to exclude European powers from the Western Hemisphere under the Monroe Doctrine. Isolationism, which assumed that the United States could ignore considerations of European power politics while pursuing its national objectives, in fact presupposed a specific balance of power, based in part on Britain's maritime superiority; unaware of this, we were led by tradition and experience to interpret international affairs in terms of Locke's notion of the relations between free individuals in an essentially peaceful state of nature.

Our involvement in World War I was therefore quite consistent with the frame of mind underlying an isolationist policy. We could believe that our intervention was necessary to preserve the freedom of the high seas—a principle that Americans view as a reasonable international law (if not a reasonable law of nature); we did not have to think of ourselves as attempting to restore a global balance of power. This attitude explains the easy return to isolationism in the 1920's; for having exorcised the threat of German violations of our neutrality, we could assume that a peaceful world order would once again be restored without our active day-to-day concern.

The United States has therefore become fully conscious of its status as a world power only since World War II. Even during this war, many felt that the defeat of the Axis would permit a new return to "normalcy"; only the exhaustion of Great Britain and the rest of Europe, combined with the threat of Communism based in the U.S.S.R., made it evident that our presence in Europe was necessary to preserve the peace. Those who realized, before the end of the war, that we would play a continued role in world politics tried to minimize the necessity through the creation of the UN; later, when Soviet hostility indicated that the international organization would be paralyzed by great-power disputes, we hastened to establish NATO as an institution that would defend the West against attack and assure us of peaceful dealings with our European allies.

Our willingness to act as a great power has thus coincided with a determination to base our involvement on formal institutions that regularize the relations between states. In the 1950's, we entered into a series of so-called "collective security" treaties: after NATO came the ANZUS and SEATO pacts, as well as a host of bilateral treaties. What has derisively been called the "pactomania" of John Foster Dulles is, however, merely an extension of the Lockean principles widely accepted by Americans: when one's security is threatened by the degeneration of peaceful relations into a state of war, the natural solution is to establish formal institutions. In more recent years, the same reflex has been apparent in proposals to settle differences of interest within NATO by the establishment of a multilateral force or a consultative committee on nuclear strategy, on the assumption that reasonable allies need only establish common institutions within which they can settle their mutual differences.

Our attitude toward the UN as a global organization is thus similar to our view of regional institutions joining allies against a common enemy (like NATO, SEATO, or the OAS). Americans have described both as institutions protecting the "collective security" of member states; in the American mind support for the UN and for NATO is completely consistent. Hence we have fled from the brutal realities of power politics even in playing the role of a world power: whether in the era of isolation or in the present day, our tendency is to avoid any conception of foreign affairs based primarily and decisively on the need to manipulate a balance of power between rival states. Transposing Locke's conception of domestic politics onto international relations, we instinctively responded to the continuous threat of war by establishing international organizations supposedly capable of resolving conflicts peacefully (on the model of our own federal government).

It may be thought that the connection between our commitment to international collective security and our attitude toward domestic political institutions, framed as it is in Lockean terms, has been exaggerated. Yet in an important diplomatic exchange with the President of France, Lyndon Johnson wrote:

> Let me begin with the American conception of the purpose of the North Atlantic Treaty and the alliance it creates. Under our Constitution the treaty is the law of the land. Like our Constitution, it is more than a

legal document. It is the outward and visible form of a living institution
—not an alliance to make war but an alliance to keep the peace.[14]

Here one sees clearly the American image of an international alliance that
is tolerable because it mirrors our view of domestic society; treaties that
are oriented to making war are presumably evil, for they reflect the transient
needs of power diplomacy rather than a community having "a political
integrity and an identity of interests," based on "bonds of culture, of political institutions, traditions, and values."[15]

The insufficiency of this attitude can be quickly perceived if one com-
pares the North Atlantic alliance and the United States Constitution. Under
NATO, each member state has the legal right, on or after April 4, 1969, to
denounce the basic treaty and leave the alliance; it is hard to imagine the
remaining members attacking a state that utilizes this privilege in order
to force it to return to the Atlantic community. This was of course exactly
what Lincoln did when the South seceded from the Union in 1860, for the
United States is a single nation, not an alliance of sovereign states. That our
federal system is also composed of units called "states" should not blind
us to the fundamental difference between Virginia and France; international politics is an arena of independent societies whose governments have
a legal right to make or break alliances whenever they find it in their self-
interest to do so.

It may now be somewhat easier to show why Americans are peculiarly
accustomed to speak in moralistic terms when discussing foreign policy. As
has been remarked, our actions are ultimately pragmatic, being based on
what appears to be the most effective response to the problem at hand (be
it the incursions of Indian tribes, the desire of slave owners for new territories to the west, or the Kaiser's unreasonable sinking of American ships
on the high seas). This approach to external affairs has been eminently successful, but only because it has seemed to us legitimate and right;
the Lockean principles so widely accepted on our shores have been used to
justify whatever action our leaders chose in order to solve immediate problems to our best advantage.

---

[14] *The New York Times,* March 25, 1966, p. 7.

[15] See President Johnson's address to the Foreign Service Institute, quoted in *The
New York Times,* March 24, 1966, p. 18. This address repeats the comparison between
NATO and the U.S. Constitution used in the letter to President de Gaulle and explicitly
refers to "the design of collective security protecting the entire Atlantic community."
Popular opposition to admitting Peking to the UN rests on the similar assumption that
UN membership, like participation in NATO, represents a wholehearted acceptance
of commonly shared political principles; for most Americans, the UN Charter is a
social contract in the Lockean sense.

Locke's principles of the natural equality and freedom of all men not only encouraged the self-reliant attempts to solve problems on the part of individuals; they also counseled governments to abstain from undue interference in private affairs, thereby permitting the acquisitive passions of man to contribute to the strength and power of the community. In the American context, therefore, Lockean traditions and pragmatism went hand in hand, allowing us to combine forceful political rhetoric (which in Europe was usually the sign of ideological rigidity and impracticality) with inventiveness and a spirit of political compromise. This may explain the apparent contradiction between the fundamentalist or Puritan tone of American Protestantism and the self-seeking if not corrupt activities of American businessmen; similarly, it suggests why the passion of political oratory throughout the nineteenth century (which often surprised European observers) did not produce a social revolution like those on the continent.

American pragmatism was of course not primarily oriented toward international affairs. Charles Pinckney echoed the thoughts of many Americans (then as now) when he told the Constitutional Convention:

> Our true situation appears to me to be this: a new extensive Country containing within itself the materials for forming a Government capable of extending to its citizens all the blessings of civil and religious liberty—capable of making them happy at home. This is the great end of Republican Establishments. We mistake the object of our Government, if we hope or wish that it is to make us respectable abroad. Conquest or superiority among other powers is not or ought not ever to be the object of republican systems. If they are sufficiently active and energetic to rescue us from contempt and preserve our domestic happiness and security, it is all we can expect from them; it is more than almost any other Government ensures to its citizens.[16]

Yet in a setting that led men to equate international affairs with a normally peaceful state of nature, this pursuit of "domestic happiness" led to an industrial progress so astonishing that we have now attained "superiority among other powers" without having established it as our "object."

Our straightforward use of persuasion and power has been rewarded by history in no small part because it has rested on confidence and self-reliance, which in turn has depended on an unquestioning acceptance of our popular beliefs about human nature and politics. As Tocqueville noted, nineteenth-century Americans did not seem given to philosophic reflection. America's rise to the status of a world power thus rested, perhaps necessarily, on a fail-

---

[16] Solberg, *The Federal Convention*, p. 169.

ure to understand the peculiar conditions that made our approach to political life so successful. Because the United States refused to enter into "entangling alliances" on the European continent, we were free to expand, using force where necessary; as in Locke's state of nature, we acquired property and power by means of our labor and initiative.

Since the vital interests of other major powers were not challenged by the foreign wars in which the United States engaged during the nineteenth century, the costs of erroneous policies were minimal. However, now that we have been forced to play the role of a world power, Americans are confronted by a tension between their traditional pragmatism—entailing as it does the uninhibited use of force to remove external obstacles—and the hazards of nuclear war. For this reason, it is of particular relevance to consider the major example of a short-range foreign-policy decision that had catastrophic consequences for the United States. In so doing, we may discover why both the traditional distrust of power politics and the moralistic rhetoric that often accompanied it are today extremely dangerous.

The American "Balance of Power" and the Civil War

The Civil War represents the only occasion on which American institutions proved incapable of resolving domestic conflicts; the debate concerning the injustice of slavery could not be settled by compromise and delay because it became clear that either the North or the South would come to dominate the Union as a whole. Each section sought to impose its interests and conception of justice on the other, and neither was willing to tolerate defeat. As some have argued, civil war was inevitable once Lincoln posed this problem boldly in 1858 by declaring that "this government cannot endure permanently half slave and half free."[17]

It was not, however, totally inevitable that the American Union collapse on the issue of slavery; many of the Founding Fathers had expected this "peculiar institution," so contradictory to the principles of human equality established in the Declaration of Independence, to wither away. Both at the Constitutional Convention and in the Missouri Compromise of 1820, our pragmatic ability to resolve immediate problems seemed adequate to settle the conflict of interest, at least temporarily. Why then did civil war result in 1860?

A strong case could be made for the proposition that the annexation of Texas in 1845 and the Mexican War of 1846-48 were the decisive links in

[17] See especially Harry V. Jaffa, *Crisis of the House Divided* (Garden City, N.Y.: Doubleday & Co., 1959).

the historical chain of events leading to the secession of the South. Once before in our history the acquisition of new lands had produced the threat of secession; when the Louisiana Purchase threatened to alter the sectional balance of power between North and South, New England Federalists talked of leaving the Union. Because the new states carved out of the Louisiana Purchase were not intrinsically bound to any one section or interest of the original states, compromise was possible; in contrast, the acquisition of Texas and the territories of New Mexico and California seemed to be solely in the interest of the slave-holding South.

It is understandable that Southern politicians sought to increase their power by extending the portion of the United States in which slavery seemed economically feasible; their ability to gain broad support for this policy is equally comprehensible, for the desire for territorial expansion, by violence if need be, was widely shared and confirmed by past American experience. But the *ad hoc* decision to annex Texas and the Southwest had long-range effects on the balance of power within the American political system; once it was recognized that the addition of many new slave states along our southern border would lead to the introduction of slavery in the territories of the Great Plains, then approaching statehood, the North saw that it was in danger of becoming a permanent minority.

The Mexican War indicates how the typically American view of foreign affairs, in which the use of force is a reflexive response to obstacles in the state of nature, can have disastrous consequences. Short-range decisions, like the annexation of Texas, led almost imperceptibly to commitments that altered the configuration of power on which the United States rested. As a result of these changes, it became impossible to compromise on the issue of slavery without effectively defeating, on a permanent basis, one or the other of the major sectional interests in American politics.

In the nineteenth century, therefore, the Achilles' heel of the American political system was the source of our power—namely, a self-confident pragmatism, resting on Lockean principles, that encouraged the use of persuasion, money, and force to secure maximum immediate advantage without reference to long-range strategies. Even the Civil War was not as disastrous as similar crises in Europe, because the resulting dominance of the North opened the way to the rapid industrialization of the late nineteenth century. The unselfconscious quest for power and wealth redounded to the economic benefit of all, including the waves of immigrants after the 1870's; whereas the French Revolution left social cleavages that were to be ignited once again by the revolutions of 1830, 1848, and 1870 (not to mention the further constitutional changes represented by the Vichy regime and the Fourth and Fifth Republics), our institutions survived intact.

One condition for the longevity of the American Constitution and its ability to survive the storm of the Civil War has unquestionably been the limited impact of world politics. The subsidiary importance of foreign affairs can no longer be taken for granted, however, because the very purpose of American commitment in world affairs has radically changed since 1950. No longer are we primarily concerned with "domestic happiness and security"; rather, as President Johnson phrased it, we have come to believe that the cause of freedom is "indivisible" throughout the world.

This shift has been an unforeseen result of foreign commitments that, following American experience, were practical responses to immediate crises. But now that the United States has embarked on a new role as a world power, the responsibilities involved can be expected to create vigorous domestic controversy. Moreover, the resulting debates probably will become increasingly bitter, for each side defends an aspect of our national traditions.

Those who insist that the threat of world Communism be met with force where persuasion fails are in effect responding to America's status as a global power in the same way that our leaders acted in the nineteenth century; just as President Polk dispatched troops to occupy parts of Texas contested by the Mexicans and President McKinley ordered the fleet into Manila Bay, so President Johnson did not hesitate to send American troops to the Dominican Republic and South Vietnam.

In contrast, those who feel that they have yet to reap "all the blessings of civil and religious liberty" at home argue that the domestic objectives set forth by Pinckney in 1787 should be fully achieved before we spend billions in defense of the South Vietnamese. For the American Negro and the most vocal supporters of the civil-rights movement, the social consequences of the Civil War should be remedied before we attempt to win the cold war by exporting the "Great Society" to foreign lands.

It is to be feared, therefore, that the unplanned role of world power will place extraordinary strains on American political life. However one judges the particular issues as they arise, the central problem lies in the persistence of the traditional approach to foreign affairs. As long as we treat international affairs as we have in the past, there is great danger in the contradiction between current conditions and the Lockean notion of a peaceful state of nature (which occasionally requires the use of force against the unreasonable and less civilized enemy).

Adequacy of the Lockean Perspective

Re-examination of the adequacy of our political traditions as they apply to international politics is therefore today indispensable. The principles of John Locke, which explain our insistence on each American citizen's natural right to "life, liberty, and the pursuit of happiness," have also colored our perception of foreign affairs; our national experience has led us to consider world politics as if they were domestic affairs. Just as every reasonable man should be aware that private property is a natural right that cannot be replaced by socialism, so reasonable statesmen should abide by certain international laws. If they do so, the peaceful accommodation of political differences among states, like the peaceful state of nature among reasonable individuals, need not degenerate into a state of war.

This approach to world politics assumes, as Locke does, that it is possible to understand political rivalries in terms of the rational calculations all men are likely to make. But this notion of human reasonableness is open to an important objection. Locke treats the "law of nature" as a set of rules that will be agreed upon by equitable men who think alike; his principles seem universally applicable. Yet in fact his political doctrines have had great impact only in the Anglo-Saxon world; the conception of man's natural rights took a very different form in the French Revolution of 1789, and private property has never been as sacrosanct on the continent as in England and the United States. In part, this is due to historical accident; the connection between democracy and local self-government, so strong in our own traditions, has been largely absent in European societies, where democratic governments could only be established by the revolutionary overthrow of a highly centralized monarchical government.

Constitutional democracy in Western Europe has therefore developed along lines that frequently diverge from our own experience. Not only have central governments been more powerful on the continent, but the principle of the separation of powers has been less well established; in contrast to the two-party systems of England and the United States, European democracies have most often had a large number of parties, not to mention a conception of the parliament as the sole representative of the people. The Bonn regime in West Germany is perhaps the most striking exception to—and confirmation of—this generalization, for the new German constitution was largely a conscious imitation of the Anglo-Saxon model, adopted during our military occupation.

It is therefore dangerous for Americans to assume that our political principles are totally shared by other democratic nations. Even apart from Communist states, most other countries do not share our conception of what is reasonable or unreasonable. Leaving aside the English (and some former British colonies like Canada and Australia), our attitude toward war and peace is relatively unique; most statesmen do not expect that international conflicts can be resolved if rivals negotiate in good faith, for they are aware —if only from their own domestic experiences—that agreements will often be violated whenever individuals or groups have the power and self-interest to do so.

Our moralistic denunciations of Communist aggression, for example, must strike statesmen like General de Gaulle as rationalizations that justify our pursuit of America's national interests. The more we refuse to see the depth of this divergence of assumptions, the more others feel that we seek to establish our hegemony over them; since we consider reasonableness as agreement with our notion of reason, governments that view the world from very different perspectives cannot help but distrust or misunderstand us. Lacking our belief in the principles of John Locke, they naturally doubt the sincerity of our actions based on these principles.

This fundamental gulf between the moral and political principles of nations cannot be ignored, nor can it be attributed to the stubbornness of our allies and the hostility of the Communists. On the contrary, men are social animals who naturally live in groups; it is natural to distinguish between those who are part of one's own society and those who are aliens. Moreover, it is characteristic of virtually every human society that it inhabits a territory which it will, under threatening circumstances, defend against outside attack.[18] The philosophical principles of John Locke are not confirmed by modern science, for the rise of society cannot be attributed to a social contract concluded between previously isolated men. Hence it becomes vital to reinvestigate our own traditions with a full awareness that many of our assumptions about foreign affairs are neither shared by others nor necessarily valid.

It is by no means easy to alter commonly held opinions that have been the basis of generations of political experience. Indeed, it may be simply impossible for Americans, having acted upon views that reflect Lockean principles, to subject these principles and opinions to searching criticism. This is particularly so because Locke's political teaching has a peculiarity that it shares (surprisingly enough) with Marxism.

Marx's political ideas have one characteristic that contributes to the tremendous effectiveness of Communist ideology: he claimed to have dis-

[18] For a popular statement of the ethnological evidence concerning human nature, see Robert Ardrey, *African Genesis* (New York: Dell, 1962), and *The Territorial Imperative* (New York: Atheneum, 1966).

covered a scientific theory of human history that was at the same time a guide to political practice. We fail completely to understand Communism if we do not see this unity of theory and practice, for Marx provided both an explanation of the human condition and a recipe for improving it.

The development of a scientific theory of politics that is simultaneously a practical political program should not be dismissed lightly as a minor aspect of Marxism. On the contrary, it explains the paradoxical success of Marxist principles despite the failure of Marx's own predictions. He expected that the working class in the industrialized Western democracies, spurred on by inevitable class conflicts that would produce economic disaster, would revolt against the capitalist order and abolish private property; instead, continued economic progress has led to the emergence of a welfare state combining private capital with public assistance to the less fortunate.

Although Marx's scientific predictions have thus not been fulfilled, his doctrines have successfully inspired those who initiated revolutions in Russia, China, and other economically underdeveloped countries. A teaching that was developed in the West has become the dominant ideology in the East. One curious reason for this success of Marxist ideology is that it is a Western theory that can be used to criticize the West (just as Locke's was an English doctrine used by the colonists to justify their independence from England). As such, Marxism is admirably suited to the needs of rulers who seek industrial development in imitation of the West but in opposition to Western domination.

Marxism would not, however, be such an effective ideology if it were merely a convenient vehicle for the mixture of admiration and hostility toward the West that marks the underdeveloped world. Other Western thinkers criticized their own societies but have not had the same impact as Marx. The decisive aspect of Marxism is its claim to provide the scientific truth concerning man in a form that simultaneously indicates the proper and desirable course of political action. Underdeveloped nations seek to imitate Western science, and here is a scientific doctrine, developed in the West yet critical of capitalist institutions, that supposedly outlines the route to political success. Especially as reformulated by Lenin and Mao, this fusion of theory and practice has attracted many who are frustrated by the seeming inability of backward societies to catch up to the industrialized democracies of the West.

The Lockean principles so long accepted in the United States are, on the surface, totally antithetical to Marxism. For Locke, men have a natural right to private property, and only on this basis can the just society be established; for Marx, it is through the abolition of private property that man will end the tyranny of one class over another, ushering in true human decency and justice. Despite these fundamentally divergent assumptions, Locke shares Marx's belief that the theory which fully explains political life is a tenable guide to political practice. Locke not only argued that his principles could justify the political settlement of 1688, upon which English constitutional democracy was and still is based; he also attempted to realize these principles in practice by writing the constitution of the colony of South Carolina.

Locke's theory is intended to be fully consistent with the realities of life (as is Marx's); beginning from the desire of every man to preserve himself, Locke tries to show how the natural laws of human behavior can be channeled into prosperous and stable societies. His emphasis on limited government according to the law is intended to realize, in practice, the truths of philosophy that he attempted to establish for all time. There is a sense, however, in which Locke's principles presuppose that men will be aware of their natural rights; if they continue to believe that kings rule by divine right, Locke indicates that the proper limits on civil society will be difficult if not impossible to establish. As we have seen, Locke must ultimately assume that all men—or at least all members of a just society—share the same view of reason and understand the same laws of nature.

History shows that Locke's principles are not held by all men. They have, instead, become the ideology of the Anglo-Saxon, or at most the Western, democracies. Rather than establish a theory that applies without question at all times and all places, Locke developed a set of ideas that characterize certain societies as distinct from others—and, most particularly, as distinct from Communist states. This occurred because Locke sought to have a direct effect on contemporary politics; unlike Plato, whose description of the best political order in the *Republic* is presented as virtually impossible to achieve (and hence as a proposal that will be laughed at), Locke seriously tried to set forth principles that could justify and govern day-to-day political practice.[19] On this score, if no other, Locke and Marx seem to share a common view that a scientific theory of human nature can lead to a feasible program of action.

The persistence of international rivalry gives rise to doubts about the sufficiency of both the Marxian and the Lockean attempts to develop a philosophy that is simultaneously a practical guide to statesmen. It seems that

---

[19] Compare the Preface to Locke's *Two Treatises of Government* with Plato's *Republic*, 473 C-D, 502 C, 592 A-B; and Plato's *Laws*, 736 B, 778 B, 858 A-C. Aristotle stated clearly the view of the classical Greeks: "It is evident that philosophic wisdom and the art of politics cannot be the same" (*Nicomachean Ethics*, 1141a).

such an attempt produces instead an ideology that is inevitably opposed by other ideologies. On the deepest level, it is the necessary incompleteness of any set of popular political beliefs, including those most Americans accept unquestioningly, which leads the observer to insist that an effective foreign policy must be oriented to a balance of power. In this sense, our political traditions and national experience may have ill-prepared the United States for its new role as a major world power.

KENNETH W. THOMPSON

Normative Theory in International Relations

International relations is a subject of growing importance because life and death issues hang in the balance. At one stage in history, it was no more than intellectually stimulating to study the relations among nations, empires, and rulers. Today, a drama of awesome proportions is being played out on the world stage. The survival not only of men and nations but of mankind is at stake. The struggle for power is inseparably linked with the struggle for existence.

In measuring the consequences of national policies or objectives, the observer is bound sooner or later to invoke value questions. What is the value, for example, of a nation's independence as compared with the value of peace? What is the relative value of forestalling aggression or slowing down the arms race or building anti-missile defense systems or emphasizing butter rather than guns?

Every time the student raises a basic question of ends or means in the realm of war and peace, he very likely (whether implicitly or explicitly) is posing a value question. He is making normative assumptions, formulating

Kenneth W. Thompson, formerly a member of the political science faculties of Northwestern University and the University of Chicago, is currently active in educational administration and the development of universities in new nations. He is the author of *American Diplomacy and Emergent Patterns, Political Realism and the Crisis of World Politics,* and *The Moral Issue in Statecraft;* and the co-author of *Principles and Problems of International Politics, Man and Modern Society, Foreign Policies in a World of Change, Conflict and Cooperation Among Nations,* and *Isolation and Security.*

positions regarding good or bad, better or worse, evil or more evil; and there are important benefits to be gained from bringing this fact to consciousness, both for him and for those who rally around. He should be willing to apply tests of reason, history, consistency, context, relevance, and priority to the position he espouses. More often than not, however, he excuses himself from this discipline and defends his position on the basis of authority, precedent, necessity, or law—leaving to his critics a broad area for debate. They take their stand on grounds he has long since passed over in his thinking. This explains why the ultimate norms on which current thinking is based are hidden or obscured. The current debate on Vietnam, the recurring discussion of emerging crises, and the historic controversy about internationalism and nationalism all reflect to some degree this absence of genuine dialogue.

Obstacles and Possibilities of Normative Thinking

In part, the avoidance of normative debate stems from a prevailing emphasis on facts. Most foreign-policy issues—ratifying a treaty, approving a customs agreement, accepting a program of cultural exchange, issuing a visa, trading or not trading with friend or foe—involve painstaking judgments in a narrowly defined realm of fact. What are the "facts," for example, concerning the rights of a corporation to engage in business abroad? The original premise is generally lost sight of, left unexamined, or assumed because policy-makers operate, and indeed must operate, within an established framework. They assume, and from an operational standpoint are obliged to assume, that the facts to be determined are circumscribed and relatively simple in character. They are determined, as a rule, in terms of a specific checklist: What is national policy? What are the credentials of the firm? Has an invitation been issued? Does it have the capacity to operate abroad? What will its actions do for the national interest, etc., etc.? Rarely, if ever, are the underlying issues appraised, such as the relation of international business to the building of a more lasting peace, or the fostering of a healthier economy or a stronger polity abroad, or the priorities of such an endeavor in terms of a set of national and international priorities. There are certain stubborn obstacles in the makeup of international society that militate against using a scale of values as the basis for approving or rejecting concrete proposals concerning business, politics, or education abroad. When individuals and corporate bodies venture abroad, they do so not as the result of moral evaluations but from the standpoint of narrowly practical choices. Not ultimate right or wrong but questions of workability and practicality are normally controlling.

The environment in which international morality must be practiced is largely determined by profound underlying forces such as individualism and nationalism. Moral action involves individual choice, and the narrowing areas of individualism limit the sphere of moral choice. The great choices seem to involve collective action. The solitary individual thus resigns himself to a state of powerlessness on the significant decisions of the day. The problems and issues are so complex and difficult that individuals are prone to conclude that they can contribute little to their solution. Men come to see themselves as objects rather than subjects of social and political action. In such a setting, the question of a just society loses its urgency. The individual who stands in danger of losing his identity also finds his moral concern weakened by a mass age.

Similarly, the force of nationalism tends to weaken the sense of solidarity men feel with the suffering and persecuted elsewhere in the world. Principles of right and wrong must be channeled through national agencies and interpreters. Here the domestic and international scene have certain analogies. With the former, programs of social welfare involving slum clearance and housing, help to the sick and aged, and widening opportunities for the poor and disadvantaged follow laws of rational organization. A vast machinery of social action has been instituted with the aim of serving the needy individual. If the "Good Samaritan" of our day wants to help someone, he must isolate himself more and more from those he wants to help behind a whole gamut of administrative machinery. It is obvious that those instruments are abstract and dehumanized; indeed, this is the condition of their effectiveness. Acts of love and compassion must be made part of an administrative case load. The great challenge in a collective era is discovering the human significance of anything that might otherwise become just another case. Organized social action hovers dangerously near the brink of the routine and procedural. The one antidote is remembering that the system's justification is the individual. This attitude and spirit must penetrate the organized structures of social action if deterioration and decay are to be avoided.

On the world scene, the need for a civilizing and informing moral attitude is equally urgent. In international affairs it is difficult to talk about ethics in general or to single out national policies that are wholly and unqualifiedly good. Nor is it always clear that on all questions in dispute the organized international community embraces justice. Those national leaders who declare that the United Nations, for example, embodies what is right and moral may, when confronting issues vital to the national interest, find their conception of justice at odds with the UN's. The real issue in debates over political ethics usually arises in the realm of means, not ends. This is why it is difficult and often pointless to talk about ethics in general, whether in terms of peace, justice, or international order. Decisions in foreign policy seldom involve simple and tidy choices. Actions stem from on-balance judgments. What is usually called for is an evaluation of the elements involved in a decision and the consequences likely to flow from each alternative course of action. In choices that are made, the best may be the enemy of the good. Not absolute truth but practical morality must be the guide.

In Jacques Maritain's words, "Means must be proportioned and appropriate to the end, since they are ways to the end, and, so to speak, the end itself is in its very process of 'coming into existence.'" Such a view of foreign policy must give heed to the call for restraint, to a sense of proportion and prudence. With John Dewey, we can say that "means and ends are two names for the same reality." Proximate morality may be the highest attainment in statecraft.

The focal point of moral purpose in international relations is the interests and goals of a nation. We start with the tacit assumption that responsible men will, broadly speaking, view national interest in similar terms. If this were not so, bipartisanship would be impossible. The present Secretary of State has observed that he has appeared before the committees of Congress in executive session more than two hundred times. He is able to recall only two occasions when the discussion of important issues was cast in partisan terms. On both sides of the aisle the controlling viewpoint was "what is right for the country." Congressmen off the hustings seek the best interests of their country. The Englishman T.H. Healy wrote to Lord Hugh Cecil, "Nationalism is what men will die for. Even the noble Lord would not die for the meridian of Greenwich." If the national interest does not exhaust the possibility of ethical principles, it is always the necessary starting point.

This fact should never obscure the need for a decent respect for the opinions of mankind. If it is possible for political leaders to think responsibly about the national interest, they can also be expected to search for common interests with the spokesmen of other nations. If national interest is a fact, so is the mutuality of national interests. There are common interests transcending narrow national interests. They form a network of shared relationships that draw together men of different national creeds and aspirations. For example, Germany today is sharply divided into opposing political systems. No one expects the differences between East and West Germany to dissolve overnight. If change can be expected it will come from a series of little steps or technical changes that may draw the country together or encourage a political settlement. Trade, cultural exchange, and limited tourism may, if practiced with patience and restraint, unlock the doors to greater unity. Even when existing political systems divide, common social, cultural, and economic interests may in time serve to reunite them.

No division is more profound and no cleavage greater than that separating the present rivals in the arms race. Looking out over the chasm that divides East and West, the late Secretary-General of the United Nations, Dag Hammarskjold, put forward a design for disarmament by "mutual example." He asked whether the Soviet Union and the United States did not have a common interest in limiting armaments and checking their spread to other powers. History will show that the great powers have inched ahead in the limitation of armaments. Bilateral disarmament in certain fields preceded the nuclear-test-ban treaty. There have been tacit agreements to limit at certain points the further accretion of various forms of military preparedness. There has been in recent years a corresponding respect by both sides for territorial boundaries in Western and Eastern Europe. Although there is still no overall peace settlement for World War II, the crises in Hungary and Cuba demonstrated a tacit acceptance of the other side's hegemony in its own sphere of influence.

Finally, international society is not bereft of certain broader principles of justice, freedom, and order. Their form may be embryonic in a half-organized world, but their existence is understood. In formulating their foreign policies, states seek points of correspondence between what they do and the broader principle. In foreign policy the concept of elemental right and wrong is never fully realized, but it can be approximated. Even the fact that states possess an awareness of injustice indicates the possibility of justice in foreign affairs, for a sense of injustice presupposes categories of justice to which leaders have recourse. Anti-colonialism is firmly rooted in certain general and inchoate notions of what is right. Often the right is but dimly perceived. Frequently, distributive justice is the highest attainment of states. The right may be as hazy and unclear as the shadows of Plato's cave. Yet these shadows are the beginnings of the necessary conditions for greater justice in the relations between states. As Reinhold Niebuhr has observed, "Our position is not an enviable one. Yet from an ultimate standpoint it need not be regretted. For a nation which cannot save itself without at the same time saving a whole world has the possibility of achieving a concurrence between its own interests and the general welfare; which must be regarded as the highest form of virtue in man's collective life." Order is the framework for the healthy growth of viable nation-states. A respect for national independence demands an international order to safeguard it. Freedom and justice presuppose order. If the world and its staunch supporters cannot preserve the international order, an early casualty is bound to be the survival of new and independent states.

Thus, there are layers of ethics in politics and international affairs. They deserve attention and study, especially since the strongest voices are those of crusaders and cynics. The ethical dimension comprises shades that are not black and white. Grays predominate; indeed, the distinguishing characteristics of political ethics are found in the recognition of the relativity of all ethical judgments. The centers of morality and religion in the land cannot stand aside from man's needs in this realm. For example, the church that teaches patience in all things should strive to inculcate this attitude toward world affairs. Foreign policy all too often is like a woman's work—it never ends. As every long-suffering housewife knows, even freezers and dishwashers have not changed this fact. In much the same way, the shining UN buildings, multilingual translation facilities, and instantaneous communications systems around the world have not prevented one challenge or conflict from following close on another.

The consequences of actions that were noble in themselves are seldom fully anticipated. For example, a well-deserved homeland for suffering and persecuted Jews has led to new tensions in the Middle East. The French Revolution brought in its wake Napoleon's armies on the move across Europe. Independence for the newer nations in our day is only the beginning of new trials and testing. "It is provided in the very essence of things," Walt Whitman declared, "that from any fruition of success, no matter what, shall come forth something to make a greater struggle necessary." Most of life is lived on the ground of successive crises. Peace and prosperity in an "America sailing on a summer sea" never provided the acid test of character. Rather, moral and spiritual resources are put to the test when peoples or nations teeter on the abyss of disaster, or when decisions have to be made for which there is neither present consensus nor future certainty. Ethical judgments, however painful and difficult, often reach a high point in clarity and resolve at the moment of moral crisis.

The Evolution of Normative Thinking

One approach to international relations that has enjoyed public and scholarly attention is that of policy-oriented research. Respected institutions like the Brookings Institution have over the years contributed a steady stream of policy studies concerning various areas of the world.

Normative Theory in International Relations

One criticism of policy research has been that it is primarily value-free research. Scholars assume a degree of detachment denied the hard-pressed decision-maker. They enjoy a greater measure of freedom and a broader range of options than policy-makers. Choices that are conceivable for detached observers are often unthinkable for those whom the public holds accountable as guardians of the national interest. National values provide the framework for rational decision-making; standards for judging good and bad foreign policy are fixed by evolving conceptions of the national interest. A national statesman who justified policy by proclaiming that it served wider international goals at the expense of vital national interests would not long continue as his country's representative. The norms of a foreign office, however vaulting the values its spokesman affirms, must in the end be tested by their responsiveness to national security and national interest.

The normative emphasis in international studies in the aftermath of World War I derived from another source and reflected another perspective. In its early days as a separate discipline, international relations was reformist in outlook and dedicated to remedying international anarchy. The failure of the Senate to support the creation of the League of Nations was taken as an object lesson; it spurred American scholars to devote themselves to the task of laying the foundations for building an effective international organization. The purposes of the first chairs of international study were described in these terms. Occupants were to help create a climate of opinion favorable to new international institutions. The directives of scholars were therefore not primarily scientific. They had a mission: to assure that what had occurred with the repudiation of the League would not occur again. If scholarly writings often took on a moralistic and legalistic flavor, this was the underlying reason. International relations had a purpose and a norm, defined fairly simply and unequivocally as building "a commonwealth of nations." What contributed to this goal was viewed as positive and good, what detracted from it as negative and bad.

This version of a normative approach had certain undeniable strengths and virtues. It gave to the new discipline of international studies a definite and rather uncomplicated focus. It assisted university leaders in making clear-cut judgments on the requirements for filling new academic posts in an emerging field of study. Indeed, in the interwar period the overwhelming majority of professors in the field were authorities in one of two closely related "disciplines." Their major concern was either with international organization or with international law. Their chairs were so designated, and their writings and research reflected this emphasis. They undertook to prepare the way, successfully as it turned out, for a new system of international institutions.

While the normative view of international relations has continued into the present, interpreters and scholars have chosen to deal with more complex and less malleable realities. If the objective of the early stages of normative thinking was straightforward and simple, it grew more sophisticated and pragmatic in later phases. This can be made clear through stating the objectives of the two periods. The early objective was "peace through organization"; later it became "peace and justice through the convergence of interests, organization, and power."

Normative thinkers in recent times have felt constrained to look at international realities through bifocal lenses. On one hand, the development of an international community is, as earlier thinkers had proclaimed, indispensable to national survival in an interdependent world. On the other hand, nationalism is possibly the most stubbornly persistent reality of our time. It acts as the channel and, sometimes, as the transforming agent for worldwide ideological movements. It reshapes Communism to fit Russian, Chinese, and Yugoslav patterns. It may sometimes be disruptive, disorienting, and evil. It can also be constructive, integrating, and unifying. The once simple dichotomy of bad nationalism and good internationalism that prevailed in the early stage of normative writing is no longer sufficient. Communism is a world-wide internationalist movement seeking to remake the world in its image. How does the normative interpreter evaluate this form of internationalism alongside, say, the process of nation-building in newly independent states? Is it not too simple to cast the world in good and evil categories when most developments shade off into questions of relative good or evil for a particular moment in time?

Moreover, recent contributions to normative thought have set out to demonstrate that values and norms, like men and states, are plural and not single. Norms for groups and nations, like norms for individuals, are multiple and interrelated. Clarity and the beginnings of wisdom are not necessarily achieved through simplicity. This can be seen in any evaluation of the policies of a given state. The United States today is dedicated to "peace through international organization." It also espouses the goal of justice in the world. How are the goals of peace and justice to be maintained? What resolution is possible if they conflict? What if these norms, which are clear as general directives, point to conflicting policies in practice? When is the norm of peace to be pursued at all costs and at the expense of justice, and when is justice to be the paramount goal in guiding the conduct of the United States? How are norms affected by technology and by the means of destruction? Is it true that the norms of international order and justice, which were supreme in a pre-nuclear era, must be sacrificed to the pursuit of peace in the nuclear era?

There are other issues that arise for the normative thinker. What influence does the stage of development of a nation-state have on the legitimate goals it holds and defends? Is isolationism or neutralism defensible for colonial America and newly independent India but indefensible for Britain or the United States today? How do we distinguish between guiding principles for rich and poor nations? Can we draw a line between, say, the use of force that runs counter to the principles of the UN Charter and its employment in maintaining the unity of a threatened nation-state?

In short, students and observers who have written about norms in international society since World War II have placed far greater emphasis on circumstances and the situation. They have tried to relate norms to context, and have put greater stress on the preconditions for viable rules and effective institutions than did their precursors following World War I. Their approach reflects, if you will, greater concern with the link between ethics and context; they are children of a trend of thought that some have described as "situational ethics."

International law as an expression of normative thinking reflects a similar emphasis. It looks at international obligations through spectacles that relate the conduct and behavior of states to forces and circumstances. Today's international lawyers are more likely to ask questions like these: "What are the circumstances under which treaties and commitments are most likely to be observed?" "When will these obligations be set aside or bypassed, and when will they be transferred to larger international bodies?" Charles de Visscher, Wilfred Jenks, and Philip Jessup all have provided examples of this approach. So do the participants in projects sponsored by the Ford Foundation that are trying to establish links between the legal superstructure and the economic and political infrastructure in various societies.

Thus, normative thinking is still an important feature of international studies. It has lost none of its significance, nor is it any less central to the purpose and direction in which states and the world are moving. The temper and orientation have been altered, however: the spirit is more likely to be analytical and critical than crusading. Fortunately, able minds have been at work in each period of the developing study of international norms. Contributions in this area have helped to clarify the nature, structure, and framework of the working international system.

Vietnam as a Case Study in Political and Normative Thinking

The dialogue between those who support and those who oppose American policy in Vietnam flounders on conflicting moral assumptions. The acceptance of one or another premise leads inescapably to mutually irreconcilable moral and political conclusions. One trend of thought draws on historical and legal arguments that justify the defense of South Vietnam in the name of the commitments of four American Presidents. A nation's word is its bond, and our promise to come to the aid of a Southeast Asian country whose independence is threatened must be observed. Otherwise aggression unchecked at it source will spread and lead to a general conflagration, as in World War II. The other trend of thought puts the stress on the civil-war characteristics of the struggle. It condemns American policy-makers for intervening in an internal struggle, arguing that the major conflict was and is between local factions organized around the National Liberation Front and the government of South Vietnam. It points to the carnage and bloodshed that follow in the train of warfare once it breaks out and expands. The debate between these two viewpoints is unlikely to yield to arguments that are at odds with first premises.

Whether we like it or not, Americans are faced with what Dean Acheson was wont to call a factual situation. We are engaged in what has become a large-scale effort to resist a military and political invasion from North Vietnam. Whatever the elements of the struggle may have been at the outset, they now involve the movement of men and equipment from North Vietnam into South Vietnam. Our government and seemingly the majority of the American people are committed to turning back the troops led by four leading North Vietnamese generals in the South. On Christmas Day, 1966, two full-scale North Vietnamese divisions crossed the 17th parallel into South Vietnam. Eight hundred small craft moved down the coast the moment the air truce was announced to supply fighting men in the South.

What are the moral and political principles relevant to the "factual situation" this conflict has engendered? Two that come to mind—restraint and the use of diplomacy—are in the realm of means. They fall in the area Maritain described in declaring that means must be proportionate to ends. Critics who denounce and "view with alarm" run the risk of ignoring the partial "good" of policies in this area. This has been true for the Korean War, the British defense of Malaya, or American policy in Vietnam.

Restraint in politics or war can be a moral precept, and it is not an inconsiderable gain that the struggle in Vietnam remains a limited war. With the possible exception of some of the bombing in the North, American responses have been limited and measured. The Administration, all too conscious of the risks of a thermonulcear holocaust, has not expanded ground operations to the North. It has resisted calls of an often more belligerent Congress for all-out war and bombing in the North. It has held in check the spread of war fever and hysteria. Much as was done in nineteenth-century international politics, it has allowed the conflict to be circumscribed. In effect, a ring has been thrown around the belligerents and every effort has been made to resist the spread of the conflict. Indeed, the help of our major rival in the cold war, the Soviet Union, has been sought to limit the spread of the conflict.

Second, diplomacy has marched hand in hand with military activity. Strenuous and unremitting efforts have been made to explore ways for setting in motion peaceful processes that might bring the belligerents to the conference table. Every available diplomatic channel has been explored, sometimes admittedly with more compulsiveness than success. Meanwhile, endless discussions have gone on with the Soviet Union on other matters. Often unnoticed, significant advances have been made on such things as cultural exchange, trade, and the signing of the space treaty. Today the Soviet Union and the United States stand on the threshold of both a nuclear proliferation treaty and a consular treaty. Fifteen years ago, Winston Churchill hammered incessantly on the necessity of arming not to fight but to parley. The Administration has not lost sight of this advice, even though its achievements here must be measured more by deeds than by clear articulation.

A third moral and political principle that is relevant in a conflict-ridden world is the need to define the political objectives that inform and inspire a military conflict. Historically, the United States has fallen short of full clarity in formulating its goals. In World War I, the best Woodrow Wilson could do was to declare that our war aims were "to make the world safe for democracy." The diplomatic debacle at Versailles followed. In World War II, the goal was "unconditional surrender." The military conflict ran its course with the resulting division of Europe that carried the seeds of the struggle with the Soviet Union. Once more in Vietnam, little has been said that contributes to the cessation of conflict and the achievement of a peace. Many people doubt that the United States would expend the amount of blood and treasure pouring into South Vietnam if we did not plan to stay after the war. We have not been explicit about our political objectives and the kind of a political order in Southeast Asia that would be acceptable once the conflict came to an end. For example, what are our hopes for political cooperation among the states in the area? What is our goal for the status of the former Indochinese states? Would we accept a neutralization agreement internationally endorsed or guaranteed? What is our view about the withdrawal of air bases from the mainland of Asia? What kind of a defense perimeter do we have in mind? What do we see as our political objectives vis-à-vis China? Isolation? Containment? Or limited cooperation at some stage, say in curbing further nuclear proliferation?

There are limited steps of a moral and political character that are "imaginable" even in the depths of international rivalry and conflict. It is unfortunately the case that these partial "goods" are less appealing to moralists than are towering moral ends that comfort and reassure the conscience but leave the "factual situation" essentially as it was.

Normative Theory: Its Status and Opportunity

The complexities of the international scene and the urgency of current problems heighten the need for normative thinking. It would be reassuring to say that the literature abounds with serious writing on normative problems. The truth is that discussion of normative problems appears to lag both in status and prestige. It does not figure extensively in listings of research awards. Its spokesmen constitute no more than a handful of observers. Numerically superior by far are the so-called value-free social scientists. Behaviorist approaches to international-relations theory are currently in vogue. Nevertheless, the need for serious and exacting normative thinking is ever more clear. How can it be advanced? What is needed to spur first-rate minds to pursue such thinking? What qualities must an observer bring to the task?

First, the normative thinker must be prepared to take the long view of his subject. Normative thinking, like politics, is the slow boring of hard boards. It is less a matter of affirming the good than of probing for complex interrelationships between objective principles and hard facts. This effort may call for a marriage, or at least a sympathetic mutual awareness, of philosophy, history, and the social sciences. The philosopher and theologian are more likely to illuminate objective truths, and the historian or social scientist to explore empirical facts. To combine these skills, whether through one mind or many, is the first step in developing normative theory.

Second, every intellectual discipline has its tests that must be applied in studying problems. Normative thinking is no exception. The laws of philosophy and history apply. Normative thinking based on bad philosophy or bad history will not make a lasting contribution. At the same time, neither the traditional concerns of philosophy nor those of history will answer the need. A blending of interests and questions is called for, requiring traditionalists and students of contemporary issues to join hands.

In all this, the relevant guidelines include the tests of reason, history, and context. Attention must also be paid to relevance, continuity, and priority. Each guideline is surrounded by a body of experience that contributes to its usefulness in normative thinking. The task is to apply and translate rules and precepts more commonly associated with other fields. Rigorous study and analysis is the overall requirement.

The laws of reason bear on moral evaluation, especially when issues of international politics and diplomacy come into play. Writings on political reason make up a worthy chapter in the annals of political science. The guiding principle of reason assumes that ordering concepts can be chosen for relating otherwise independent events and data. Political reason historically has been associated with "reason of state." The observer proceeds with a rational map that sets out the course an independent state can be expected to follow in its national interest. The map assumes rationality on the part of policy-makers. It asserts not that all states at all times will adhere to the dictates of political reason but rather that a national imperative toward self-preservation will inform a nation's policies. In the long run, neither ideology nor visionary leaders are likely to override the hard demands of national interest. The moralist who sets out to plot the course a nation should follow cannot ignore the hard demands of political reason.

Likewise history and the traditional and geographic position of a nation must influence its moral and political outlook. Foreign policy is a product of the elements that determine a nation's position in the world. For example, the continuity of postwar American foreign policy is not the result of political uniformity or common membership in an elite or in *the* establishment. Presidents Roosevelt, Truman, Eisenhower, Kennedy, and Johnson came from different regions and social classes. They differed in temperament and outlook, and it would be difficult to equate their understanding of the world. Yet across all differences of experience, viewpoint, and party their foreign policies in the end were remarkably similar. The historic objectives and traditional interests of nations influence the shape of their external relations.

The context in which moral goals are pursued sets the framework for normative discussions. It is tempting to approach moral questions in general terms; their importance for normative theory is found in the concrete situation. For the statesman, his personal sense of right and wrong must accommodate to the demands of public responsibility. For President Lincoln as an individual, the practice of slavery was morally reprehensible. As the nation's chief executive, however, he was obliged to measure what he asked the nation to do by its effect on the union. Thus he declared that if he could preserve the union by freeing all the slaves he would do so; if the union could be preserved by freeing none of them, he would do that; or if he could save it by freeing some and leaving others as slaves he would do that. The test was the effect on the union. The President by his oath is pledged to defend and preserve the union, and in this context public morality overrides personal morality. That the two may conflict is well illustrated in certain Asian countries where continuing responsibility for meeting familial needs may clash with a leader's public trust.

Moral precepts must also be relevant. Law and justice more readily take form in an integrated society with effective machinery for lawmaking. Where institutions and community are lacking, legal prescriptions can be irrelevant. The problem in international society is the lack of widely accepted moral principles on which legal structures can be built. Philosophers have defined proximate morality as a body of mediating principles grounded in objective principles but more attuned to the given realities. Distributive justice is such a mediating concept that outlines working precepts of practical morality.

Finally, priorities must be drawn up both in general terms and for specific situations. It will not do to make an absolute out of a particular moral concept. The true situation with moral principles is that the actor in world affairs must choose not between good and evil but among competing moral principles. Justice may be a moral concern in one circumstance, while peace may take priority in another. Security is sometimes the controlling interest, while freedom may prevail at other times. Someone must formulate a scale of moral values relevant to given circumstances but subject to application under differing circumstances.

The point is that normative thought in international relations must pay heed to the guidelines of responsible analysis. The shape of international society—half organized and half anarchic—sets the framework. It would be as unreal for the moralist to ignore this as for the military analyst to overlook military realities. The opportunities for serious normative thinking rest on a full awareness of the elemental rules and guidelines for analysis.

Third, students of values must be prepared to deal with ambiguities and impalpables in much of their work. Thanks to logical positivism and modern analytical philosophy, some value questions can be dealt with precisely and in quantitative terms. For other facets of normative thought, the interplay of contingent, unpredictable factors and the tragic clash of conflicting values limit certainty and sharp definition. In this sphere, the most we can do is surround a problem, box it in, and point to the alternatives. The best writings on moral choice appear murky to the scientist or mathematician, but this results less from lack of clarity than from the intrinsic nature of the problem. The solitary individual, whether in personal or public life, is unlikely to face his dilemmas of moral choice through a mathematical equation. Rather, he will solve them existentially through trial and error, testing and probing, using his senses as well as his reason. A leading college president said recently, "I've seldom made the wrong decision when I trusted the feeling in my bones." This element of choice is not readily categorized; it resists simple generalization or transferability. Those who would recognize normative thinking in its full dimensions must take this into account.

These three aspects of the approach to revitalizing normative theory need further discussion. They are at most a part of the basic considerations germane to theorizing. Perhaps even this broad statement can help to suggest for others those aspects of intellectual activity unique to value study and those that bind it to other forms of humanistic and social-science study.

293

1866